WHETHER YOU ADMIT IT OR NOT

THE CRAFT OF SALES

WHETHER YOU ADMIT IT OR NOT

A Field Manual for the People Who Sell for a Living— and the People Who Don't Realize They Do

DAVE DASS

21-YEAR SALES DIRECTOR · VACATION OWNERSHIP INDUSTRY
LICENSED REAL ESTATE & MORTGAGE BROKER

Whether You Admit It or Not: A Field Manual for the People Who Sell for a Living—and the People Who Don't Realize They Do

This book reflects the author's recollections of experiences over a career in sales. Names and identifying details of buyers, colleagues, and others have been changed to protect privacy. Certain individuals and events are composites created for illustrative purposes. The stories are offered to teach the craft, not to document any specific person or transaction.

The information in this book is provided for general educational purposes. It does not constitute legal, financial, or professional advice. The author is a licensed real estate and mortgage broker but is not acting in that capacity in this book, and nothing herein should be construed as advice for any specific transaction or situation.

Edited and typeset by Liz Kazandzhy, www.WatchfulWordsmith.com

First Edition
Published in the United States of America

Paperback ISBN: 979-8-9969646-0-4
Ebook ISBN: 979-8-9969646-1-1

https://books.by/dave-dass

For Jenny, who never asked me to choose something safer —

and for Dane, Charlene, and Shannon —

and for Noah, Liam, Kaiden, Paris, and Thomas —

and for Stephen, Tommy, and Kana —

the years we get.

CONTENTS

Part III: The Technology

AUTHOR'S NOTE

From the Floor

This book was written from a sales floor.

Not from a research desk. Not from a corporate training department. Not from a podcast studio or a consulting practice or a business school. From the carpet between the chairs where the buyer and the closer sit down across from each other, ninety minutes on the clock, a contract in a folder between them, and one of two things about to happen.

I have spent the last twenty-one years on that carpet.

Most of those years were as a sales director at one of the country's largest vacation ownership developers. The job is harder than it looks from the outside. The product is real, the contracts are real, and the buyer is sitting across from you in a state of suspicion that the entire industry has earned through decades of its own worst actors. The good salespeople on those floors are some of the best practitioners of the craft alive in any field. The bad ones wash out fast. The middle—the reps who survive but never break out—never quite figure out why the top 10 percent keep beating them with what looks like the same script.

I almost washed out in my first month.

I was twenty deals behind board, one bad weekend away from being fired, and certain I had made a career-ending mistake. I had been trained on the script, the close, the rebuttals to every objection.

I knew the product cold. I was running the same playbook everyone else on the floor was running. But I was losing every tour I touched.

Then, the week before the end of my first month, I shadowed Joe.

Joe was the veteran on the floor that everybody quietly watched. Thirty-five years in the business. The rookies called him "the grand daddy"—half out of reverence, half out of the kind of running joke a sales floor lands on when nobody quite knows how else to talk about a closer who's been doing the work longer than most of them have been alive. He was the kind of closer the rookies were told to learn from, even though nobody could quite articulate what Joe actually did differently. I expected him to run a sharper version of the script. He didn't. From the moment he met the family in the lobby to the moment the husband signed the contract ninety minutes later, he did one thing.

He told stories.

Stories about other buyers. Stories about other families who had been in the room before this one. Stories about what ownership had meant to a couple from Kansas City the previous month, what it had unlocked for a widow whose husband had died before the trips he had been promising her, what it had meant to a father who had been able to give his son a kind of childhood he himself never had. Joe kept the family's names in the conversation from the first minute. He used the kids' names. He used the wife's name twice as often as the husband's. Because he had read the room and knew where the deal was.

He didn't pitch.

He told stories until the family recognized themselves in one of them.

Then he closed.

The family signed before they left the room. I walked out of that tour understanding something the script had never told me. People don't buy products; they buy stories that bring out feelings. They buy the experience of being seen and named and heard by someone who's paying attention to them as people. The script doesn't do that. The script *can't* do that. The script has no way of knowing that a man's daughter is twelve and named Emma, or that a woman has been postponing a trip to Italy for fifteen years, or that the couple across the table hasn't taken a vacation together since their last child was born.

But Joe knew.

From that week forward, I rebuilt my approach from the ground up. I learned to tell stories in my own voice. I learned to listen for the buyer's story before I told mine. I learned that the script was a floor, not a ceiling, and that the work happened in everything I added to the script because I had actually seen who walked in.

I never looked back. By the end of my second year, I was a top closer on the floor. By the end of my fifth, I was a director. I have spent the years since teaching the version of this craft that Joe taught me—and watching every modern sales book miss most of what he knew.

Throughout this book, I'll refer to "the sales canon"—the handful of foundational texts every working salesperson is expected to have read. Carnegie, Cialdini, Pink, Voss, Rackham, Dixon, Tracy—the seven books that shape how the field talks to itself. There are hundreds of sales books in print, but these seven are the ones a serious practitioner is expected to have engaged with, and the ones a serious book about sales is expected to take seriously.

I take them seriously. I also disagree with them where the floor disagrees with them. When the canon and the floor diverge in this book, the floor wins.

Joe was running Carnegie's playbook from 1936—names, genuine interest, listening, talking about what mattered to the other person—without knowing he was running Carnegie. He had never read the book. He didn't need to. The floor had taught him directly what Carnegie had described eighty years before.

That is this book's central observation. The canon is downstream of the floor, not the other way around. The best books in the canon—Carnegie above all—are valuable because they describe accurately what working salespeople have been doing for centuries before the books were written. The weakest parts of the canon are weak because the authors theorized from outside the work, in domains they hadn't lived in long enough to see clearly.

This book audits the canon from the inside.

I take Carnegie at full strength on the warm-up. I push back on Rackham about which axis his data actually measured. I credit Voss for naming the moves veterans had been running for forty years before he wrote his book. I argue that Cialdini undersells what happens when all seven of his principles are stacked at industrial scale on a tour floor. Each of these arguments is grounded in twenty-one years of watching what the books described—and watching what they missed.

I still sell.

I am a licensed real estate broker and mortgage originator in Orlando, Florida. I have been brokering real estate since 1994—over thirty years in that market through every cycle the modern era has produced—and writing mortgages for the last five. The craft of vacation ownership selling and the craft of mortgage origination are not the same craft—they live in different quadrants of the matrix that you'll meet in Chapter 1—but the underlying work is recognizable across both. The buyer is still a person. The trust still gets built early or it doesn't get built at all. The story still does most of the heavy lifting.

I'm writing this book now and not ten years ago for a specific reason. Artificial intelligence has begun to collapse parts of the sales profession that have been stable for decades. Reps who used to do an honest day's work prospecting and qualifying are watching their jobs get automated in real time. New reps coming into the field are being trained on tools that their managers don't understand. The salesperson of the next decade will look different from the salesperson of the last one, in ways that have not yet fully resolved.

A book written now has a chance to name what's changing and what isn't. The craft itself—the human-to-human work of moving another person across the decision they've been carrying—is the part of the job that doesn't collapse. The tools *around* that are collapsing fast. Salespeople who understand the difference will thrive. The ones who don't will be replaced by tools built by people who do.

This book is for the ones who want to thrive.

A note on the stories that follow.

Names and identifying details of buyers and colleagues throughout this book have been changed to protect privacy. The stories themselves are real. The deals happened. The people existed. The lessons are what I learned from them, told in my own voice, with the specifics altered to keep my buyers and former colleagues out of a book they didn't sign up for.

Joe—"the grand daddy"—was real. The widow whose husband had been a physician was real. The teenager who was supposed to be on vacation and turned out to be a serious golfer was real. The hesitant wife who took three weeks to feel safe was real. The reps who washed out and the ones who survived were all real.

What follows is what they taught me.

— Dave

INTRODUCTION

Why You're Reading This (Whether You Admit It or Not)

Make a list.

Write down every time in the last seven days you tried to convince another human being of something. Every time. Not just the obvious ones—not just the meetings, the negotiations, the proposals, the calls with clients or customers if you have those. All of it.

The job interview you went on. The raise you asked for (or wish you had asked for). The vacation you talked your spouse into or out of. The bedtime you negotiated with your kid. The restaurant you steered the group toward. The first impression you made on the stranger at your daughter's school. The way you positioned yourself in the family text thread before bringing up the thing nobody wanted to talk about. The pitch you made to your own boss for a project, a budget, a hire. The reasoning you offered your aging parent for why they should consider the move you have been gently pushing for the last six months. The email you redrafted four times before sending because you knew the recipient was going to decide something based on how you framed it.

Count them honestly.

Most readers will hit fifteen before lunch.

Here is one I'll keep thinking about.

A pediatrician walks into the exam room. The mother is sitting in the chair against the wall. The little girl is on the exam table, swinging her legs, looking at the wall instead of at anyone. The mother is rigid. The doctor recognizes the posture immediately. She has seen it a thousand times. The mother has been preparing a *no* in the parking lot, in the elevator, in the waiting room, in the chair against the wall.

The doctor doesn't open with the procedure.

She kneels so she is eye-level with the girl and asks about the unicorn on her shirt. The girl tells her the unicorn's name. The doctor tells the girl that her own daughter is exactly the same age. The mother watches all of this without saying anything. After two minutes, the doctor stands up and turns toward the mother, and she does not begin with the medical case for the procedure.

She begins with a question: "What are you most worried about?"

The mother starts to cry.

The fear is not the one the doctor was prepared to address. The fear is something specific—a sister who had something similar at this age and a memory the mother has been carrying for thirty years.

The doctor doesn't interrupt. She doesn't reassure prematurely. She doesn't pivot to the medical case. She lets the mother finish the story, and when the mother is finished, the doctor does not respond by minimizing what she just heard.

She names it.

She says, "That is the thing you've been carrying into this room. I understand now."

The mother nods. Something in the room has changed. The fear is no longer between them. It's on the table where they can both look at it.

Then the doctor does what the chart didn't predict she would need to do. She doesn't pitch the procedure. She separates what happened to the sister thirty years ago from what's going to happen to this little girl this month. She explains—slowly, in specifics, without medical jargon—exactly how the conditions are different, exactly what the procedure involves, exactly what the outcome is for children at this age with this presentation. She is not selling. She is *informing the version of the mother who is now able to hear information*—the version that was not in the room ten minutes ago.

The mother asks two questions. The doctor answers both. The mother asks a third. The doctor answers that one too.

The procedure gets scheduled.

The little girl is fine.

The doctor would be insulted to be called a salesperson. But she is one of the best ones I have ever watched work.

This is the part of the book where most authors write a paragraph that starts with "In today's fast-paced economy" and continues for three pages about how the world has changed. I am not going to do that.

Because the world hasn't changed.

What has changed is that we now use the word *sales* for a smaller and smaller fraction of the work it has always described. The car salesperson is the salesperson. The mortgage originator is the salesperson. The realtor is the salesperson. The retail closer at the watch counter is the salesperson. The pharmaceutical rep, the recruiter, the lobbyist, the investment adviser, the timeshare rep on a Saturday afternoon—all of them are the salesperson, and all of them carry the title.

The schoolteacher convincing a board to fund the program is not called a salesperson. Neither is the doctor explaining why a treatment is worth the cost, the pastor making the case for the building expansion, the nonprofit director writing the grant application, the therapist persuading the patient to try the harder homework, or the mother explaining to her teenager why the consequence is fair.

But the work they're doing is the same work. They are moving another person across a decision. They are trying to change what someone else believes, wants, or is willing to do. They are making the case for something against the alternative of nothing.

That is sales.

Most of the people doing that work would be insulted to be called salespeople. They have inherited, somewhere along the way, the assumption that the word *sales* belongs to a narrower and slightly suspect activity—the act of getting someone to part with money for a thing they may not actually want. They want no part of that activity. They distance themselves from the title.

And yet the craft they're practicing every day—the work of moving another person across a decision—is the same craft the salesperson on the tour line has been practicing for two hundred years. The only difference is that the salesperson knows what they're doing. The teacher, the pastor, the therapist, the mother, and the doctor often do not. They've been doing the work without the framework—sometimes well, sometimes poorly, mostly by feel.

This book is for all of them.

In 2012, a writer named Daniel Pink published a book called *To Sell Is Human*. His central claim was that something like 40 percent of American work time was now spent in what he called *non-sales selling*—the work of moving other people that didn't carry the title of sales but did the same thing under different names.

Forty percent.

That number is now fourteen years old. The fraction has since gone up, not down. The rise of remote work, the collapse of stable middle-management hierarchies, the platform economy, the gig economy, the always-on culture of professional persuasion that runs on LinkedIn and Slack and email and Zoom and a dozen other channels that didn't exist in their current form when Pink was writing—all of it has expanded the territory. There is less of the old kind of work and more of the new kind. And the new kind is selling, even when nobody calls it that.

The people who recognize this are at a structural advantage.

Not because they're more aggressive or more manipulative or more *salesy*—those are caricatures of the craft, not the craft itself. They are at a structural advantage because they have a framework for what they're doing. They can name the moves. They can see the conversation they're in. They can adjust when something isn't working, because they have the vocabulary to identify what's not working and the toolkit to try something else.

The people who refuse to recognize this—the teachers, doctors, pastors, parents, nonprofit directors, and creative-class professionals who would rather not think of themselves as salespeople—are doing the same work with one hand tied behind their backs. They are running by feel. Sometimes by very good feel. But they have no framework, no canon, no vocabulary, and no community of practice.

This book is for both groups. The ones who sell for a living and want to get better at it. And the ones who don't sell for a living, who think they would never be caught dead reading a sales book, who picked this one up out of curiosity or because someone handed it to them, and who are about to discover that the work they've been doing for fifteen or twenty years has a name they've been avoiding.

This is not a motivational book.

It's not going to tell you that you can sell anything to anyone if you just believe in yourself. It's not going to tell you that you're a closer who has been hiding from your destiny. It's not going to give you scripts you can memorize and run in your next conversation. It's not going to convince you that sales is easy or noble or virtuous. Sometimes it's all of those things, but often, it's none of them.

This is a field manual.

That phrase—*field manual*—is doing real work in the sentence. A field manual is what a craft produces when it's been around long enough that the working practitioners have agreed on what is true. It's written from inside the work. It's short on theory and long on what has been observed to actually work in the rooms where the work is done. It's meant to be carried. It's meant to be referred to. It's meant to be argued with by the next generation of practitioners who add to it from their own experience.

The book you are holding is a field manual for the craft of moving another person across a decision, written from twenty-one years inside that work.

A few things about the architecture, so you know what you're walking into.

The book has three parts. The first is the *craft*—the lived practitioner work of sales as veterans have always understood it. Presence, rapport, questions, storytelling, the read of a room. The second is the *science*—the research and theory the sales canon has produced over the last ninety years, audited against what the floor actually teaches. The third is the *technology*—the tools and platforms and artificial intelligence that have begun to rewrite the job in real time, and what every salesperson has to understand about that shift now.

Each chapter ends with a field drill—a specific thing you can run this week to test the chapter's argument against your own work. The drills are the point. The chapters are scaffolding for them.

Throughout the book, I'll refer to "the canon"—the sales literature that working practitioners are expected to have engaged with. The Author's Note covers what I mean by that term. If you haven't read it, do that first. The framework won't make sense without it.

You will also meet, repeatedly, a few people. Joe—"the grand daddy"—who taught me in my first month that people buy stories, not products. Rick—a closer who taught me twenty years later that the sale starts before the customer opens the car door. Margaret, who walked her own life through a tour after her husband died. Karen, who took three weeks to find her way to a yes. Noah and Hank Dawson, who showed me that the right question in the first ninety seconds is worth more than any pitch I have ever delivered. Their names have been changed, but they are all real.

The lessons are not changed.

Also, a quick word on what this book is not.

It is not a memoir. The stories are here to teach, not to record my career. I am not the protagonist—the buyer is the protagonist. The salesperson is the second character in the scene, usually arriving late and leaving early. The book's arc is what I have learned from twenty-one years of watching buyers across tables, not what I personally accomplished. If you came looking for a victory lap, you have the wrong book.

It is not a book against technology. I run AI tools in my own mortgage practice every day. I think anyone who tries to sell in the next decade without using them will be left behind. The chapter on AI is not a warning; it is a working description of the stack as it stands in 2026 and a forecast of where it's going.

It is not a book that pretends the sales profession has been entirely honest. The vacation ownership industry has produced some of the worst sales practices in American commercial history. So has mortgage lending. So has automotive retail. So has investment advising. The bad actors in every one of those fields have done real damage. The book doesn't pretend otherwise. What it argues is that the craft itself—done with skill, honesty, and respect for the buyer—is still one of the most useful human activities there is, and that the way to fix the bad actors is not to abolish the craft but to teach the next generation to do it better.

It is not a book that thinks every reader will agree with every chapter. I disagree with the canon in several places. The careful reader will disagree with me in several places. That is what a working field manual is for. The book is meant to start arguments, not to end them.

One last thing before we begin.

The fifteen times you tried to convince someone of something this week—the ones you wrote down at the start of the introduction, or noticed in your head if you didn't write them down—those moments are why this book exists.

You are already doing the work.

The question this book is going to help you answer is whether you want to keep doing it by feel for another decade, or whether you want to put a framework around it now and watch what happens to your conversion rate. Not your sales conversion rate, necessarily, but the conversion rate of the rest of your professional and personal life—the rate at which the things you're trying to convince other people of actually happen.

I have spent twenty-one years on the floor watching people do this work well and badly. I have watched the difference it makes. The reps who put a framework around what they were doing climbed. The reps who refused to learn the craft stayed where they were.

Those are the same two outcomes available to you.

Start where you want.

The first chapter is *The Real Axis*—the framework that organizes the rest of the book. After that, *The Tour Begins When They Pull In*—what Rick taught me about the parking lot. And after that, *Names, Kids, Vacations*—what Joe had been doing the whole time, finally explained.

Then we go to work.

— D.

PART I

THE CRAFT

CHAPTER 1
THE REAL AXIS

A husband and wife arrived at the resort one afternoon expecting a simple tour.

They were drawn to the property immediately—the grounds, the units, the quiet weight of what ownership looked like up close.

They were the kind of guests who understood value the moment they saw it. But they were also the kind of guests who didn't make large decisions on the day they were introduced to them. They had told me as much before we sat down.

So I told them a story.

A few months before, I had walked a woman through the same tour. Her late husband, Dr. Walter Reilly, had been a physician—the kind of man who worked himself to the bone, promising her year after year that one day they would take the vacations they had been talking about since they were young. He kept the promise in his head. But he never kept it in the calendar.

He died before any of those trips happened.

Margaret came into financial independence through the inheritance. More money than she had ever had to think about by herself. And she came to the resort, on her own, because somebody had mentioned ownership to her and she wanted to understand what it was.

She didn't buy a vacation that afternoon.

She bought *intention*.

Two units. Four weeks a year. The structure forced the calendar to honor the promise her husband never had time to keep. From that day forward, four weeks of the year were already spoken for. They couldn't be given back to work, or to errands, or to one more thing that needed doing. They belonged to her, and to the version of her life she had stopped letting herself live.

I told my couple that story while sitting on the model unit's balcony.

They were quiet for a long moment after I finished. The husband looked at his wife. She was already looking at him.

They bought a package before they left the property.

Not because I had pressed. Not because the day's pricing was about to disappear. Because somewhere in Margaret's story, they had recognized their own postponed life, and they had decided—together, in the space of an afternoon—that they didn't want to be the people who waited too long.

That is a transactional close.

Ninety minutes from handshake to signature. One sitting. One decision. One playbook.

A few weeks later, a couple sat across from me on a different kind of deal.

Mark was ready. He had run the numbers, talked to his accountant, walked the property, and arrived at our first meeting prepared to move. He wanted to buy.

Karen, on the other hand, was scared.

She didn't say so in those words. She said it in the careful way she asked questions, in the small pause before each answer she gave me, in the way her body angled half a degree toward the door even while Mark was leaning forward across the table.

I knew the close was sitting right there on the desk between us. Mark's signature alone could have ended the meeting. In a different industry, in a different deal structure, that's how it would have ended.

But I didn't take it.

I had learned by then that when one partner is afraid and the other one is ready, the deal you close that day is the deal that comes apart later. The hesitant partner rescinds. The ready partner resents the other one. The relationship between them takes longer to recover than the deal took to die.

Nobody wins.

So I slowed down.

I told them I'd rather come back next week than rush a decision this big. Mark was surprised—I think he expected me to push. Karen exhaled. I watched her shoulders drop two inches.

That gap was the whole deal.

Over the next three weeks, I met with them twice more. The conversations weren't about price. They were about the things Karen was actually afraid of, which she hadn't articulated even to Mark until we had the room and the time for them to surface.

What if their income changed?

What if they lost the home?

What if the payments became something they regretted?

The fears weren't unreasonable. They were the fears of someone who had grown up in a household where money felt unstable and who had carried that uncertainty into adulthood without ever having a reason to put it into words.

The work wasn't pitching. The work was education.

We talked about the difference between rent and equity. We talked about how the tax structure worked, not as a sales point but as a long-form explanation. We talked about what would happen in each of the scenarios she was afraid of, what the actual exposure was, and what the actual options would be. By the end of our second meeting, Karen had asked me harder questions than Mark had thought to ask in the first one.

By the third meeting, she was leading the conversation.

And by the time we signed, Karen was the one explaining the deal to a friend on the phone in the lobby afterward.

That close took three weeks.

It was the same dollar range as a vacation ownership tour, but it was a fundamentally different transaction.

If I had run Margaret's playbook on Karen—same-day, narrative-driven, leaning on emotional alignment to compress the decision—I would have closed nothing. Sure, Mark would've signed, but Karen would've rescinded by Tuesday. The deal would have died inside the cooling-off window and taken the relationship with it.

And if I had run Karen's playbook on Margaret—three meetings, slow education, multi-week patience—she would have left the property that afternoon and never come back. The intention she felt would have dissolved on the drive home. The deal would have died of cold.

Two deals.

Same dollar range.

Opposite playbooks.

This is the chapter where we figure out why.

What the Canon Got Wrong

For forty years, the most cited finding in sales literature has been Neil Rackham's 1988 conclusion that closing techniques hurt large sales.

Rackham's work was real. He recorded 35,000 sales calls. He counted the moves. He measured the outcomes. He published the results. And his finding was true—closing pressure, applied to the deals he was studying, produced worse outcomes than soft-touch consultative work.

But Rackham named the wrong axis.

He called it "small versus large sales." The big idea of *SPIN Selling* was that small sales and large sales required different playbooks, and the dividing line was dollar amount. Small sales—the kind a sales rep closes in a single interaction—could tolerate closing pressure. Large sales—the kind that took weeks or months—could not.

The field accepted this and built forty years of training programs on top of it.

The field was wrong.

The real axis isn't size. It's *structure.*

Margaret's purchase was a large sale. It was tens of thousands of dollars. It closed in ninety minutes with a story and a balcony view. Karen's purchase was the same dollar amount, and it took three weeks of patient work to land.

Same dollar amount. Opposite structures. Opposite playbooks.

Rackham's data was telling him something real, but he interpreted it through the lens he had access to—corporate B2B sales, which happen to be both *large* and *complex*. Because the two variables moved together in his sample, he conflated them. He called the axis "small versus large" when what he was actually measuring was "transactional versus complex."

Forty years of sales training have been built on the conflation.

It's why the timeshare industry runs hard closes on multi-thousand-dollar contracts and prints money doing it. It's why enterprise SaaS reps who try to hard-close $5,000 annual contracts get walked from the room. It's why mortgage originators who treat first-time buyers like a tour-line close lose the deal, and why mortgage originators who treat refinance customers like a six-week consultative engagement lose the deal too.

The dollar amount has almost nothing to do with it.

What matters is whether the deal is transactional or complex.

The Real Axis

A *transactional sale* is a deal that closes inside a single coherent decision window. The buyer arrives in one frame of mind. The deal lives or dies inside that frame. If the buyer leaves the room, the frame collapses, and the deal usually goes with it.

A *complex sale* is a deal that has to survive time. Multiple meetings. Multiple stakeholders, present and absent. Multiple frames of mind that the buyer passes through between the start of the conversation and the close. The deal has to be alive at the end of all of them.

Two sales of the same dollar amount can sit on opposite sides of that line, because the line isn't drawn by money—it's drawn by structure.

Three things determine structure:

- **The Number of Stakeholders Who Have a Real Veto:** One person can make a transactional decision. Two people who agree can make a transactional decision. Two people who disagree, or any group of three or more, is a complex sale by default. Not because of the number but because the conversation now has to happen between the stakeholders themselves, and that conversation usually happens after you leave the room.

- **The Presence of an Absent Decision-Maker:** A buyer with an accountant they trust, a spouse who isn't in the room, an investment committee, an aging parent whose opinion matters—anyone whose voice enters the deal between meetings turns a transactional sale into a complex one. The accountant doesn't have to be in the room. The fact that the accountant *will be consulted* is enough.
- **The Buyer's Relationship with the Decision Itself:** Some decisions can be made in a single emotional frame. Others require the buyer to live with the question for a while. A vacation purchase, even a large one, can usually be made inside one frame. A first home, even a small one, usually cannot. That has nothing to do with money. It has to do with what the decision *means* to the buyer's life.

Margaret's purchase had one decisive stakeholder, no absent decision-makers, and a relationship with the decision that her late husband's death had already prepared her for. Structurally transactional. The close happened in one sitting because the structure permitted it.

Karen's purchase had two stakeholders who were not aligned, her own internal absent stakeholders (her family history, her sense of safety), and a buyer whose relationship with the decision required time. Structurally complex. The close took three weeks because the structure required it.

The dollar amount in both cases was roughly equivalent.

The playbook was not.

The Matrix

Two axes. Four quadrants.

Horizontal axis: **dollar amount**. Small on the left, large on the right.

Vertical axis: **structure**. Transactional on the top, complex on the bottom.

	SMALL DOLLAR	LARGE DOLLAR
TRANSACTIONAL	Quadrant 1 Retail. E-commerce. Restaurant. Most B2C under $1,000.	Quadrant 2 Timeshare. Auto. Most luxury B2C. Single-decision-window purchases at scale.
COMPLEX	Quadrant 3 SaaS subscriptions. Most B2B under $10K. Small consultative.	Quadrant 4 Enterprise B2B. Mortgages. First homes. Major construction. Anything with a committee.

The canon was built on Quadrant 4. That's where Rackham worked. That's where Dixon and Adamson worked. Most of the books a serious salesperson has read on their shelf are about Quadrant 4 selling, even when the cover doesn't say so.

The vacation ownership industry—the industry where I learned to sell—is Quadrant 2. Large dollar, transactional structure. A playbook that looks insane to a Quadrant 4 reader because everything about it violates the rules they learned from Rackham. And yet a $10 billion industry runs on it, every weekend, in every resort market in the country.

Tracy was right about closing pressure—for Quadrants 1 and 2.

Rackham was right about closing pressure—for Quadrants 3 and 4.

Both writers thought they were describing sales. Each was describing the half of sales they could see from where they were standing.

This is the chapter the canon never wrote because no single author has worked in all four quadrants long enough to compare them.

What Goes in Each Quadrant

- **Quadrant 1—Small, Transactional:** A meal. A drink. A retail item. An impulse purchase. The playbook is presentation, friction reduction, and a quick close. Cialdini's principles work here at full strength because the decision lives inside a single frame and never has to survive time.
- **Quadrant 2—Large, Transactional:** Timeshare. Auto. High-end retail. Many luxury purchases. The playbook is the one I ran with Margaret. Story-driven, emotionally compressed, leveraging the buyer's present frame to a close that happens before the frame can dissolve. The hard close is alive and well in this quadrant, and the books that say it died were written by authors looking at a different quadrant.
- **Quadrant 3—Small, Complex:** SaaS subscriptions. Small B2B services. Anything with a stakeholder structure that requires consensus, even if the dollar amount is modest. The playbook is patience, education, and stakeholder navigation. Closing pressure that would work fine in Quadrant 1 will kill a Quadrant 3 deal of the same dollar amount.
- **Quadrant 4—Large, Complex:** Mortgages. First homes. Enterprise software. Major construction. Consulting engagements. The playbook is the one I ran with Karen, scaled up. Multiple meetings, multiple stakeholders, education over pitching, time as an ally. This is where Rackham and Dixon-Adamson live and where their work is most useful.

The salesperson who knows their quadrant has a chance.

The salesperson who doesn't know their quadrant is running someone else's playbook and wondering why it doesn't work.

Why This Matters Now

Forty years of confusion about the axis would be a curiosity if the world stayed where it was.

But it is not staying where it was.

Artificial intelligence is collapsing the transactional quadrants. Not the complex ones—the transactional ones.

A retail purchase (Quadrant 1) is already mostly handled by an algorithm—recommendation engines, friction-free checkout, no human in the loop. That collapse is largely complete.

A timeshare-style tour close (Quadrant 2) is being squeezed from two directions. The story-driven close still works because it requires human warmth and the read of a room—but the volume of those closes is dropping as more of the discovery and prequalification work moves online. The reps who used to convert 10 percent of fresh leads are now converting 8 percent of pre-warmed ones, and the math is getting tighter every quarter.

A small B2B sale (Quadrant 3) is being eaten by self-service and product-led growth. The salesperson is increasingly an exception, not a default.

A complex enterprise or major-life-purchase deal (Quadrant 4) is the most resistant. The stakeholders, the time horizon, the emotional weight of the decision—none of those collapse easily into an algorithm. The human salesperson in Quadrant 4 is not just surviving; they're becoming more valuable. The premium for a trusted human across the table is going up.

The implication is direct. Salespeople who work in Quadrants 1 and 2 need to be making a deliberate plan, right now, for what their career looks like in five years. Some of them will be displaced. Some will move up-quadrant—into Quadrant 4 work that uses the same craft but in deals where the human can't be replaced. Some will become orchestrators of agents that do the work they used to do themselves.

Salespeople who work in Quadrants 3 and 4 need to be using AI as aggressively as possible to take over the parts of the job that *do not require* the human so that the human can focus entirely on the parts that do. The conversation. The read. The close.

This is the chapter that organizes the rest of the book. Every later chapter operates inside this matrix. When you read Chapter 2's first-ten-seconds material, you're reading Quadrant 2 craft. When you read Chapter 7's argument about closing, you're reading the difference between Quadrants 2 and 4. When you read Chapter 14's argument about AI in the sales process, you're reading a forecast of how the quadrants themselves are changing.

The reader who internalizes the matrix has a frame for everything that follows.

The reader who skips the matrix will read the rest of the book as a collection of disconnected observations.

The Field Drill

Take a sheet of paper. Draw the 2x2.

Put a dot where your work currently lives. Be honest about which quadrant—not which one you wish you were in, but which one you're actually in today.

Now do two more things.

Identify which sales books you've read. Carnegie, Cialdini, Voss, Pink, Tracy, Rackham, and Dixon. Plus anything else on your shelf that has shaped how you sell. Next to each one, mark which quadrant it was written for.

Most readers will find that more than half the books they've read were written for a quadrant they don't work in.

This isn't a small finding. It means the sales training you have absorbed over the years is, in significant part, the wrong training for the work you actually do. It doesn't mean the books are bad. It means they were written for someone else, and you have been quietly applying their advice to a different quadrant and wondering why some of it doesn't land.

Identify the next deal on your calendar. Decide which quadrant the deal lives in *before* the conversation begins. Then walk into that conversation with the playbook the quadrant requires, not the one your training defaulted to.

Most reps run their default playbook on every deal. The ones who outperform run the deal's playbook on every deal.

The difference between those two reps isn't talent. It's the frame in their head when they walk into the room.

The matrix is the frame.

Margaret bought because I ran the playbook her structure required.

Karen bought because I ran the playbook hers required.

The same playbook on either would have closed nothing.

The salesperson who understands the difference closes both.

The salesperson who doesn't, doesn't.

That is the chapter.

Next chapter: The Tour Begins When They Pull In—the first ten seconds, the read in the parking lot, and the veteran who taught me that the sale starts before the customer opens the car door.

CHAPTER 2

THE TOUR BEGINS WHEN THEY PULL IN

Chapter 1 drew the matrix. This chapter shows you what one quadrant looks like up close.

A vacation ownership tour is a Quadrant 2 sale. Large dollar amount. Transactional structure. The deal lives or dies inside a single coherent decision window, usually ninety minutes. If the buyer leaves the property without signing, the deal is almost always dead. Not because the buyer changed their mind on the drive home—although sometimes they do—but because the *frame* that made the decision possible dissolves the moment they leave the room.

That puts an extreme amount of weight on the front end of the conversation. Not the pitch—the first ten seconds.

This chapter is about those first ten seconds.

It's the most underrated piece of craft in the entire sales profession, and it's what separates the tour-line reps who make a living from the ones who wash out before their first anniversary.

Rick had been doing resort tours for almost twenty years.

Somewhere along the way, he stopped believing sales were won in conference rooms.

He used to tell the younger reps the same line so often that we could finish it for him.

"By the time you start your presentation, the customer has already told you how the meeting is going to end."

Most of them nodded like they understood.

Most of them didn't.

I watched him prove it on a Thursday afternoon.

Rick had a VIP couple on the board that day. Private tour.

When he pulled into the lot, he noticed their SUV immediately.

Brand new. Dealer tag still on it. The kind of vehicle people buy when they want the world to think things are going really well.

But the husband was sitting behind the wheel, face blank.

Engine off.

Not on his phone. Not talking. Just staring through the windshield like a man mentally preparing for something.

A few seconds later, the passenger door opened hard.

The wife stepped out first and headed toward the building without looking back.

The husband stayed in the car another moment.

Then he got out slowly. Locked the doors. Checked his watch. Looked up at the resort with the kind of face people have at a dentist's office.

That was the moment Rick quietly changed his entire approach.

The tour hadn't started. He hadn't shaken a hand. He hadn't said a word.

And he had already rewritten the next ninety minutes.

Inside the lobby, the receptionist greeted them.

The wife answered every question immediately. Almost too quickly.

The husband barely spoke more than a sentence.

Then the receptionist made a harmless comment: "Today's a great day to become an owner. We've got some exciting upgrades available."

Rick saw it instantly.

The husband gave this tiny little sigh. Barely noticeable.

But it wasn't excitement. It was exhaustion. The look of a person who already feels cornered before the presentation has even started.

If Rick had walked in with the usual hard-sell energy, the guy would have shut down completely.

So Rick did something most salespeople struggle to do.

He slowed down.

No exaggerated enthusiasm. No fake urgency. No "this deal expires today" nonsense.

About halfway through the presentation, Rick leaned back casually and looked at the husband. "You probably research every major decision for weeks before buying anything, don't you?"

The husband looked surprised. Then he laughed quietly. First genuine reaction all afternoon. "Pretty much."

Rick nodded. "Yeah. I figured if I pushed too hard today, you'd probably distrust the whole thing."

The room changed.

Not dramatically. Just enough.

The husband leaned forward slightly. The wife stopped interrupting. The tension eased.

Because for the first time that afternoon, nobody was trying to *work* him.

The conversation became real after that.

The husband started asking practical questions.

Maintenance fees. Flexibility. Resale value. What happens in retirement.

Not once did Rick dodge anything.

And when the numbers finally came out, Rick closed the folder instead of sliding it across the table.

"Look," he said. "This honestly may not be the right fit for you right now. I'd rather you walk away comfortable than regret it later."

There was a long silence. Then the husband looked at his wife and said something I've never forgotten.

"This is the first time today I feel like somebody's talking to me like a human being."

Twenty minutes later, they bought.

Not because Rick had the best pitch.

Not because of discounts.

Because he recognized something most salespeople miss.

People decide emotionally whether they trust you long before they evaluate the product. And the deciding happens early.

Most of it happens before the conversation begins.

This is the chapter the books don't write.

Most sales literature opens at the pitch.

The presentation. The script. The close.

There's a whole industry of books that walk you through the live conversation as if the live conversation is where the work happens.

It isn't.

By the time the prospect is sitting across from you, half the sale is already decided. The other half is mostly settled in the first ninety seconds you spend together, before you've said anything that matters about the product.

The pitch is the last 20 percent of the job.

The first 80 percent is everything that happens before the pitch begins.

The salesperson who doesn't understand that has a ceiling on their career that they can't see.

Twenty-one years on a vacation ownership floor will teach you that ceiling is real.

The reps who never break through it are the ones who think the job starts when they sit down at the table.

The reps who do break through know the job started when the family pulled into the lot.

This chapter is about the 80 percent.

The First Ten Seconds

The buyer is reading you before you say a word.

Your posture. Your handshake. The energy you walked in with. Whether you look like you've been doing this for an hour or twelve. Whether your shoes are good. Whether you smiled before they did or waited for them. Whether you remembered their name from the front-desk pass-off or asked for it again. Whether you addressed the wife or the husband first.

None of this is conscious for the buyer.

They're not running a checklist. They're picking up signal the way every human picks up signal in the first ten seconds of meeting a stranger.

Pattern-matching against everyone they have ever met before.

What they're matching against is two categories:

People who turned out to be trustworthy.

And people who didn't.

You don't get a vote in which category they put you in. They've already put you somewhere by the time they let go of your hand.

This is uncomfortable for newer reps to hear. The instinct is to argue with it. "I'll change their mind." "I'm good at building rapport." "They'll see who I really am once we start talking."

Sometimes that's true.

Mostly it isn't.

Mostly, the first ten seconds set a ceiling, and the rest of the conversation is you working under that ceiling.

The right response to this isn't to despair. It's to take the first ten seconds seriously.

Treat the lot, the lobby, the hallway, the handshake, the eye contact, the first sentence—treat all of it as part of the sale.

Because it is.

Dale Carnegie understood this in 1936. He didn't have the neuroscience for it, but he had the observation. The chapter on smiling, the chapter on names, the chapter on becoming genuinely interested in other people—those aren't pleasantries. They're the operating manual for the first ten seconds.

Carnegie is the first of the canon I'll engage with by name. He won't be the last. And to my mind, he gets too little credit from modern sales writers who skip his work because it sounds dated.

The floor doesn't make that mistake.

The reps who close consistently are the reps who walked in warm, present, attentive, and prepared from the second they came into view.

The reps who don't are still trying to fix something at the table that should've been fixed in the parking lot.

Rick fixed his in the parking lot.

He saw the husband's posture in the SUV. He saw the wife's walk to the building. He saw the watch check, the dentist-office face.

By the time the handshake happened in the lobby, Rick had already made three or four decisions about the next ninety minutes that the rest of the room wouldn't make for another forty minutes.

That gap is the chapter.

The Handshake

The handshake is a single second of contact.

It costs you nothing. It either earns or burns a small amount of trust.

A bad handshake doesn't lose the deal by itself.

But a bad handshake compounds.

It is one of the first three or four signals the buyer is processing about you. If it lands wrong, every signal afterward is being filtered through a slightly skeptical lens.

There's no trick to a good handshake.

Firm but not crushing. Web of the hand meeting web of the hand. Eye contact while the hand is connected, not before, not after. Use the buyer's name in the first sentence after the handshake breaks.

That's it.

What ruins it is the absence of attention.

The rep who's already thinking about the script while shaking hands is broadcasting that they aren't here yet. The buyer feels it.

If you only do one technical thing right at the handshake, do this:

Be in your body when it happens.

Feel the contact. Notice the buyer's grip. Tight, weak, hesitant, confident? That tells you something about how they walk into rooms.

Notice the eye contact. Held or broken? That tells you something about how they expect to be treated.

The handshake is information.

Most reps treat it as a formality.

Treat it as the first reading.

State

The salesperson's first responsibility is to walk in at the right level.

Veterans call this *state*. Energy, posture, breath, focus, readiness—all of it together.

You can't see your own state from inside your own head. But the buyer can see it across thirty feet of parking lot.

State is not a mood.

Mood is what happens to you. State is what you choose.

Some days, you walk in carrying things. Your kid was up all night. Your last tour walked. Your manager is on you about numbers. The market is down. Your spouse is mad.

But the buyer doesn't care. They shouldn't have to.

The buyer wants a salesperson who is fully present for the next ninety minutes. Your job is to be that salesperson whether you feel like it or not.

This is not motivational language. It's technical.

There are specific things you do to walk in at the right level.

You audit yourself before you walk out.

- Energy: Am I bringing it?
- Posture: Am I open or closed?
- Breath: Shallow or deep?
- Focus: Am I here, or am I still in the last thing?

If any of those is off, fix it before the door opens.

Cold water on the face. Walk the lot once. Five slow breaths. A song in the car that pulls you back into yourself.

Whatever works for you. Find your version and run it every time.

You also know which version of yourself the buyer needs.

A young couple on their first vacation needs warm and welcoming. A retired engineer needs precise and credible. A family with three kids in chaos needs calm and steady.

You're not changing who you are. You're choosing which true version of yourself to bring forward.

Rick's version of state that Thursday was *calm*.

Calm because the VIP husband needed calm. Needed someone who didn't add pressure to a day that had already piled it on.

A different couple on a different afternoon might have needed Rick warmer. More energetic. More direct.

He had all of those in him. He just picked the one the room needed and walked in carrying it.

State is the part of Quadrant 2 craft that doesn't translate to the other quadrants the same way. In a Quadrant 4 deal—a mortgage, a first home, an enterprise contract—state still matters, but you get more attempts at it. There's a second meeting. A third. You can recover from a flat first meeting if the rest are strong. In Quadrant 2, you get one frame. If you walk into it carrying yesterday, you lose.

The reps who don't manage state get eaten alive over a career.

Not on any single tour. You can fake state for an hour. But over a year, over five years, the cost compounds.

They show up flat when the family needed warm. They show up hot when the family needed steady. The conversion rate drifts down half a point at a time and they never know why.

The reps who do manage state look like they're always lucky.

They're not lucky.

They're choosing.

Mirroring Before Mirroring

By the time Chris Voss published *Never Split the Difference* in 2016, sales floors had been running mirroring for decades.

They just didn't call it that.

They didn't have the FBI hostage-negotiation language. They had something better—the lived instinct that when you match the buyer's pace, posture, and energy, the buyer trusts you faster.

A good rep matches without thinking.

Slow couple, slow pace. Fast-talking executive, faster pace. Quiet family, quiet voice. Loud family, more energy.

None of it is performed.

All of it is calibrated automatically by a part of the brain that learned to do this before the rep could explain it.

This is mirroring before the technical move.

Mirroring is a default, not a tool.

The technical move—repeating the last few words back, copying the gesture, matching the breath—that comes later.

It's useful in stuck conversations—a closer's tool for a stalled table—but it isn't the primary move.

The primary move is the unconscious match.

And you can't fake that with a technique. You build it by paying real attention to real people over thousands of hours.

Voss articulated something that was already on every veteran sales floor in the country. He gave it a name.

The name is useful. It lets you teach the move to someone who doesn't have the hours yet.

But the move is older than the book.

Here's what Voss got right that the older floor tradition missed.

The buyer can feel the difference between someone who's mirroring as manipulation and someone who's mirroring because they actually care.

The technical mirror without the underlying attention reads as creepy.

The buyer can't say why. They just feel something is off and pull back.

Which means you can't fake the prerequisite. You actually have to be paying attention. You actually have to be present with this family, this hour, this room.

The mirror is the output of attention, not a substitute for it.

Rick's "You probably research every major decision for weeks, don't you?" was a mirror dressed as a question.

He was reflecting the husband's posture, his caution, his careful watchfulness. He was giving him language for it.

The husband heard himself in the question and relaxed. Because someone had finally seen him correctly.

That wasn't a technique Rick learned from a book. It was the output of two decades of paying attention.

This is the part of the craft that survives every technological cycle.

AI can draft a follow-up email. But AI cannot match a stranger's breath across a table while reading the partner who hasn't spoken yet.

That is human work.

And it will stay human work for a long time.

What the Parking Lot Tells You

Back to Rick in the lot.

Before the husband was out of the SUV, Rick knew more about how the tour was going to run than the script did.

The script assumed a generic family with generic objections.

The lot told him which specific family he had and which specific objections were coming.

A man sitting still in a parked car with the engine off, staring through the windshield: This is a man bracing.

He's not on his way somewhere he wants to go. He has been brought here. Probably by the wife. Probably for a free weekend or a show package.

He has decided that he'll be polite for ninety minutes and then leave.

If Rick runs the script as written, he loses the husband at the forty-minute mark when the husband checks his watch a second time and decides that his time isn't being respected.

If Rick cuts the script—opens with an acknowledgment that the husband didn't choose this, gives him room to think, moves slower than the script intends—he has a chance.

The wife walking ahead toward the building without looking back: She wants the vacation. But she also doesn't want to be the person who pushed it.

She'll defer to him in front of Rick.

If Rick reads this and designs the conversation so the husband can say yes without it looking like she won, the deal is alive.

The dealer tag still on the SUV: Money is not the obstacle. Image is.

This family is doing well enough that the husband doesn't want to be sold to. He wants to be respected.

None of this is on the prospect card.

The card has names, ages, zip codes, and a checkbox for whether they qualify under the income threshold.

The rest is read in the lot.

A rep who walks past all that signal and starts the script the same way every time is leaving most of the job on the table.

The script is a baseline. It's a floor.

The work is everything you add to the script because you actually saw who walked in.

What the Rookies Get Wrong

The most common mistake new reps make in the first ten seconds is treating the warm-up as something to get through.

They have the script in their head, and they want to get to the pitch.

The handshake, the introductions, the small talk about the drive in—they treat all of that as friction before the real work begins.

The buyer can feel that, even if they can't name it.

The whole opening reads as performative. And the trust ceiling drops.

The veteran knows that the warm-up *is* the work.

The trust gets built in the first three minutes or it doesn't get built at all. The pitch later is downstream of the rapport now.

Rick spent the first ten minutes of that Thursday tour doing what most reps would call *nothing*. Making space. Lowering tension. Letting the husband settle. But those ten minutes paid for the close ninety minutes later.

The second mistake is leading with the wrong person.

New reps default to the spouse who looks more engaged. Usually the one who booked the trip.

That feels right, but it's wrong.

The skeptical partner is the one who will kill the deal at the table. The conversation needs to be designed for *that* partner from the first sentence.

Rick designed the conversation for the husband.

The wife was already sold. She was at the resort. She had the tickets. She wanted ownership.

The husband was the deal. So the husband got the question.

The third mistake is talking too much in the opening.

New reps fill silence with information. The problem is, the buyer hasn't asked for any of it yet.

Every word spent before the buyer is ready to listen is a withdrawal from a trust account that hasn't been opened yet.

The fourth mistake is the worst: trying to control the energy of the room by being louder, brighter, and more enthusiastic than the room is.

This reads as artificial in any setting. It reads as desperate in a setting where the buyer is already on guard.

Match the room first.

Lead the room only after you've matched it.

The receptionist's chirpy "Great day to become an owner!" was the textbook version of this mistake. Rick watched it land wrong on the husband in real time.

He spent the rest of the tour correcting for it.

These four mistakes—performing the warm-up, leading with the wrong partner, talking too much, and trying to lift the room before matching it—cost more deals on a vacation ownership floor than any technical pitch failure I have ever seen.

They are all first-ten-seconds errors.

Fortunately, they're all fixable.

Most new reps go years without anyone telling them what they're doing wrong, because the trainer is teaching them the script and not the 80 percent that comes before it.

The Veteran's Read

There's one more thing the parking lot tells you that the script doesn't.

The veteran's read is not just about the family. It's also about the moment.

What kind of day is this family having?

Are they on day one of a long-anticipated vacation, full of hope and patience? Are they on day five, tired, ready to fight about anything? Did they fly in this morning and drive straight here, jet-lagged and short? Did the GPS take them the long way and put them in traffic? Is it raining?

A family on the right day will hear a presentation that the same family on the wrong day will walk out of.

The product didn't change.

The pitch didn't change.

The moment changed.

You don't always get to pick the moment. You almost never do.

But you can read it. And you can adjust.

A short tour for the tired family. A patient one for the family that needs to settle in. A direct one for the executive who wants to be respected on his time.

The reps who can read the moment and adjust the tour to it close at materially higher rates than the reps who run the same tour regardless of what walked in.

This isn't a secret. Every veteran knows it.

It's just not in any book, because it can only be pointed at, not transcribed.

This book can point at it.

And the hours you put in will do the rest.

The Field Drill

Before your next sales conversation, run this audit.

Five minutes before the meeting—before the call, before you walk into the lobby, wherever your version of the parking lot is—stop and check.

- **Energy:** Am I bringing it? If not, what's in the way, and can I set it down for the next ninety minutes?
- **Posture:** Am I open or closed? Shoulders, jaw, hands. Reset what's closed.
- **Breath:** Shallow or deep? Five slow breaths if shallow.
- **Focus:** Am I here, or am I still in whatever happened before this? (If you're still in the last thing, you're not ready yet.)

If any of those is off, fix it before the door opens.

This is thirty seconds of real work.

Most reps don't do it because nobody told them to. The ones who do build a small structural advantage that compounds across a career.

Then, when the prospect arrives—whether they pull into your lot, walk into your lobby, or come on the line—give them the first ten seconds you would want if you were them.

Eye contact.

A name remembered.

A real handshake.

A real smile—not the one you put on.

The version of yourself you would want to meet.

Do this for a week. Then come back to this chapter and see what changed.

That evening, after the VIP couple had left with the contract, one of the younger reps asked Rick how he knew to change direction so early.

He had watched Rick run a tour that bore almost no resemblance to anything he had been trained on, and the deal had closed clean.

Rick looked out toward the parking lot and shrugged. "The sale usually starts before the customer even opens the car door."

That line is the chapter, and it's also the entire Quadrant 2 craft compressed to twelve words. The salesperson who internalizes it never runs another tour the same way again.

The next chapter takes the principle deeper—into the warm-up itself, the three questions every conversation starts with, and the part of Dale Carnegie's work that the canon undersells.

Next chapter: Names, Kids, Vacations—the Carnegie warm-up, and the three questions every tour starts with.

CHAPTER 3
NAMES, KIDS, VACATIONS

The family wasn't supposed to be vacation ownership hunting that day.

They were on vacation. Escaping the routine back home in Charlotte. Long weekend at the resort. Hank Dawson, his wife Linda, their sixteen-year-old son Noah, and a younger daughter. The kind of family that brought structure with them even on a beach trip—Hank quietly running the agenda, Noah watching everything closely, the daughter staying light, Linda holding the balance between everyone else.

The tour was a "why not." Something to fill the afternoon. The kind of impulse decision that the resort runs on and that produces, statistically, almost no deals.

I was the rep on the board.

Before the formal tour began, the group of guests was gathered near the resort's golf practice area. Casual. Unstructured. The kind of pre-tour moment most reps treat as dead time—small talk while everyone settles, then on to the script.

I noticed Noah immediately.

It was the posture. The way his eyes tracked the green when a stranger took a practice swing fifty yards off. The way he held a club he wasn't supposed to be holding—borrowed it from the rack on a whim, but his hands were already in the right grip without thinking about it.

I had played college golf myself. The body knows.

So I opened there.

"Either you play, or you've been around it long enough to fake it."

Hank smiled before Noah could answer. "He plays. Pretty seriously."

That was the warm-up.

What followed wasn't forced. It flowed. Noah stepped into the conversation, talking about training, about trying to sharpen his game for a shot at playing in college. I mentioned my own years on the team—the discipline, the grind, the part of golf nobody outside the sport understands. We traded references. He brought up Rory's tempo. I countered with Morikawa's precision. Noah's whole posture changed within two minutes. He was no longer a teenager on a forced vacation. He was talking shop with someone who took his sport seriously.

Then I asked him one question.

"Tiger or everyone else?"

Noah didn't hesitate.

"Tiger. Always."

That told me everything.

Hank laughed and started telling me how many Sunday afternoons the two of them had spent watching old Tiger highlights together. Sunday red. Pressure moments. The mindset more than the mechanics. Linda stood at the edge of the conversation now, engaged, watching her husband and son share something she didn't fully share but understood the value of.

The shift had already happened.

By the time the official tour started, I didn't need to *present* anything. The discovery the script was supposed to do in the first half hour had already been done in the warm-up. I knew what mattered to this family. I knew who the decision-makers were, in what order. I knew the language to use.

When we reached the resort's golf facilities—the practice range, the short-game area, the proximity to three championship courses—I didn't pitch features. I pitched experience. Practice conditions.

Consistency. The kind of environment where someone serious about the game could actually improve.

I tied it back to Tiger. Not the legend. The habits. Repetition. Focus. Environment shaping performance.

Noah asked questions now. Real ones, not polite ones.

Hank listened differently.

Linda, who had been quiet earlier, began to see what this place represented to her son's future—not just a vacation but a place where his goals had a structural foothold. The resort owned access to golf properties across the country and overseas. A vacation here was also a year of practice rounds at courses Noah would otherwise spend his life dreaming about.

They bought before they left.

Not because I had pitched harder than the other reps on the floor that day.

Because the first three minutes of conversation had been about Noah's grip on a club he wasn't supposed to be holding.

This chapter is about those three minutes.

The reps who never break out of mid-pack don't ever quite understand what happened on tours like that one. They tell themselves I got lucky with the family. The kid happened to play golf. The dad happened to be engaged. The match was already there before the conversation started.

That story is partly true and mostly wrong.

Yes, the match was there. But the Dawsons had been standing at the practice area for fifteen minutes before I walked up. Two other reps had passed them on the way to their own tours. Neither one of them noticed Noah's hands on the club. Neither one of them said anything to anyone in the family. The match was there, sitting in plain sight on the practice area for fifteen minutes, and the deal almost didn't happen because nobody who walked past it could see it.

The warm-up isn't luck.

The warm-up is the discipline of seeing what's in front of you and then opening a conversation that the buyer recognizes as being about them specifically.

That is harder than it sounds. Most reps can't do it. Most reps have been trained *out* of doing it. Because the training programs teach scripts, and scripts can't account for a sixteen-year-old's grip on a borrowed seven-iron.

This chapter is about how to get the training out of your head and the *seeing* back into it.

Carnegie Is Still Right

In 1936, a former salesman named Dale Carnegie published a book called *How to Win Friends and Influence People.*

It sold somewhere north of thirty million copies. It hasn't been out of print in ninety years. Almost every modern sales book that gets published in the United States is, at some level, a footnote to Carnegie—even when the modern author doesn't know that or doesn't credit him.

The canon is full of him whether his name appears on the cover or not.

And yet when I talk to working salespeople, I find that almost none of the reps under forty have actually read him. They've heard of him, but they assume his work is too old to be useful. They assume that the examples are folksy and the language is dated. They've absorbed Carnegie secondhand through every author who has built on him—and they've decided, without reading him, that he's no longer current.

This is one of the biggest mistakes in modern sales training.

Carnegie wasn't writing self-help. He was writing the operating manual for the first three minutes of any sales conversation, and that manual is still correct. The principles he named—genuine interest, names, listening, talking about what matters to the other person, sincere appreciation—are not pleasantries. They are the technical specifications for how trust forms between strangers.

The floor confirms his observations every day.

The reps who don't read him are running his moves anyway, because his moves describe how human warm-up actually works. The reps who do read him have a frame for what they're doing and can do it on purpose instead of by accident.

There are two common dismissals of Carnegie that need to be addressed directly.

The first is that his work is manipulative. "You're just being interested in people to get something from them." But this criticism misses how human relationships actually work at every level. Every introduction, every job interview, every first date, every conversation between strangers involves some version of demonstrating interest in order to build connection. Carnegie's contribution was not to invent the move; it was to describe a move that had always existed and to make it teachable. The manipulation criticism only lands if you assume the sales conversation is inherently dishonest, which is a separate argument and a wrong one.

The second criticism is that his examples sound dated. They do. He wrote for a 1936 reader who knew a different America. The wrapper has aged. But the mechanics inside the wrapper have not. A modern reader has to do the work of translating his examples into their own context. And that work is worth doing.

Where Carnegie is incomplete is not in what he said. It's in what he couldn't have foreseen.

Carnegie wrote for a world where the warm-up was the whole craft. The salesperson who could establish rapport had basically done the job. The product mostly sold itself, and the closer was rare because the buyer's deliberation cycle was measured in years for a major purchase. The warm-up was the front end of a very long arc.

Modern sales have more layers. The buyer arrives more informed, more skeptical, more aware of the rep's intentions. The deliberation cycle has collapsed for transactional sales and become more stakeholder-heavy for complex ones. The warm-up still matters—it still does the work Carnegie said it did—but it's no longer sufficient on its own. It gets you to the table. But it doesn't get you the signature.

The right way to read Carnegie today is to take him at full strength on the warm-up and then layer the modern craft on top of him.

Anyone who skips him is rebuilding his work badly from scratch.

The Three Questions Every Conversation Starts With

The warm-up is not three literal sentences. It's three *categories* of opening that the conversation needs to cover before the pitch begins.

Skip a category and the warm-up is incomplete. Run all three and the buyer is ready to be sold to. Not pressured, not pitched at—sold to. The distinction matters.

Here are the three categories, in roughly the order they tend to surface:

Where Are You From?

This is the geographic opener. Where the buyer lives, how they got here, and what kind of trip it's been so far.

On the surface, it's small talk. Underneath, it's doing several things at once.

It establishes a low-stakes topic that lets the buyer settle in without feeling sold to. It reveals the travel context—whether they flew in this morning, drove down yesterday, or have been on the property for three days. That tells you their energy reserves for the next ninety minutes. It surfaces whether the visit has gone well so far, which tells you whether they're arriving in a generous mood or a sharp one.

It also tells you something about who they are. A family from Charlotte that drove down for a long weekend is a different buyer from a couple from Manhattan flying in for the night. Both can close, but the conversation that gets them there is different.

The mistake new reps make in this category is treating it as throat-clearing. "How was your drive?" asked and forgotten. The veteran asks the same question and *listens to the answer.* The answer is the first data point in a mental file that you'll be using for the next ninety minutes.

What Does Life Look Like Back Home?

This is the family-and-work opener.

What they do for a living. What a typical week looks like. Who lives in the house. Kids, pets, parents—whatever surfaces.

This is the category that produces the warm-up's richest information. It's also the category where Carnegie's most famous principles do their hardest work: names, genuine interest, listening for what the buyer cares about and reflecting it back to them.

The names matter for a reason that's easy to miss. A buyer who has just told you their son's name and then hears that name come up forty minutes later—naturally, in context, not in a salesy way—feels seen in a way they can't articulate. They won't say to themselves, "The rep remembered my son's name." They will just feel that the rep is paying attention, and they'll start to trust the rep's read of the deal because the rep has demonstrated that the read is real.

This is also where the warm-up's diagnostic function kicks in. The buyer isn't just chatting. They're revealing what they care about, what they've postponed, what they're afraid of, what they would do if they had the means.

A family like the Dawsons, where Hank had spent every Sunday for ten years watching golf highlights with Noah, is a family that has a specific dream—Noah's golf career, the family's shared identity around the sport, Hank's quiet hope that he can give his kid a real shot. None of that came up in the script. All of it came up in the warm-up. And once it was in the room, the rest of the tour was about that dream specifically, not about the resort's amenity list.

What Kind of Vacations Have You Taken Before?

This is the product-context opener.

What kinds of trips have they taken? Where have they been? What did they love? What did they hate? Where would they go if money and time were no object?

This is the category that establishes the buyer's reference points for what ownership might mean to them. It also reveals whether they're travelers or homebodies, adventure-seekers or comfort-seekers, beach people or city people. All of that calibrates which part of the product to emphasize and which to skip.

It also tells you whether the buyer has ever had the experience your product is designed to multiply. A family that's never been to Europe will not respond to a pitch about European resort access the same way as a family that's visited twice and longs to go back. Same product, different pitch—because the warm-up uncovered a different reference point.

The mistake reps make in this category is asking the question and then steamrolling past the answer with the script. "What kind of vacations have you taken?"—"Oh, we love the beach."—"Great, the resort has beaches in seven countries . . ." The rep heard the words but missed the data. *Beach* is a category. Which beach? Why that beach? What about that beach? The answer to those follow-ups is where the actual pitch lives.

The Fourth Question—the One You Don't Ask

There is a category of question that doesn't belong in the warm-up.

Budget. Income. Credit. Whether they're ready to buy today. Anything that signals you've arrived at the pitch before the rapport has been earned.

These questions aren't bad questions. They're just questions for later. Asked in the warm-up, they burn trust that the rest of the conversation can't recover. The buyer's body language closes the moment they hear them. The rep has signaled that the small talk was performative—a check-the-box exercise on the way to the real conversation, which is about money.

The veterans never do this. The rookies do it constantly. It's one of the most reliable markers of a young rep on the floor.

If you have to know any of this information before the pitch, you find it out from the prospect card, the front-desk pass-off, the demographic data the resort already has. You don't ask the buyer.

The warm-up is the part of the conversation where the buyer is being asked about themselves. The pitch is the part where the buyer is being shown something. The moment those two categories cross—the moment the buyer feels like the warm-up has been about them being *qualified* instead of them being *known*—the deal is in trouble.

Specific Compliments Versus Generic Ones

There's one tactical move worth pulling out of the larger warm-up principle, because it gets botched constantly.

A generic compliment is a withdrawal from the trust account.

"Nice shirt."—costs you. "You guys look great!"—costs you. "What a beautiful family."—costs you. And it costs more than reps realize, because it reads as performative even when sincerely meant.

A specific compliment, on the other hand, is a deposit.

"That's a great watch—is that vintage?"—deposits (if the watch is in fact vintage). "Your son has a real grip on that club—does he play?"—deposits and opens an entire conversation. "I noticed you two finishing each other's sentences earlier—how long have you been married?"—deposits and tells the buyer you've been paying attention to them as people, not as marks.

The difference is whether the compliment proves you were paying attention or proves you were running a script.

The mistake that new reps make is *generic-compliment defaulting.* They've been trained to compliment the buyer in the first thirty seconds. But the training doesn't specify *what* to compliment, so the rep grabs the easiest thing—the shirt, the look, the family—and lands a compliment that costs them rather than earns. They usually don't even realize they're losing trust. They think they've made a deposit because they remembered to compliment.

The veteran's move is silent observation until something specific surfaces, then one calibrated compliment that demonstrates the rep was present.

If nothing specific surfaces, no compliment is delivered. Silence beats a generic compliment every time.

Where the Warm-Up Ends

This is the most overlooked craft moment in the entire warm-up.

The rep has done the work. The buyer is relaxed. Names have been exchanged. The family has shared what they do, where they live, what kind of vacations they like. The conversation is real.

Now what?

Most reps don't know how to *end* the warm-up. They either rush it—start pitching before the trust is fully built—or they extend it past its useful life, and the buyer starts wondering, politely, when they're going to get to the point.

The signals that the warm-up is over and the pitch can begin are not complicated. There are four of them.

- **The buyer asks a question about the product without being prompted.** Some version of "So how does the ownership thing actually work?" This is the cleanest possible signal. The buyer is volunteering interest. The rep has been given an explicit invitation.
- **The buyer's body language opens.** Uncrossed arms. Leaning in. Sustained eye contact. The watch checks stop. The phone stays in the pocket. The buyer has decided, somewhere below conscious awareness, that this is a conversation worth having.
- **The buyer makes a joke or volunteers personal information unprompted.** A spouse teases the other spouse. The wife mentions something she normally wouldn't bring up with a stranger. The husband laughs at something he doesn't have to laugh at. The buyer is no longer guarded. The warm-up has done its job.
- **The buyer says some version of "So, tell me more about** . . ." Even casually, even as a polite transition. They are giving the rep permission to move on.

When you see one of those signals, you move. Before then, you don't.

The mistake on one side is rushing—the rep is anxious about time, or they've internalized a script that says the pitch begins at minute fifteen no matter what, so they start pitching when the buyer isn't ready yet. The buyer feels the shift and pulls back. The trust that was building disappears, and the rest of the conversation is the rep trying to rebuild what they just destroyed.

The mistake on the other side is dragging—the rep is enjoying the warm-up, the family is engaging well, the conversation is easy, and the rep doesn't want to break the spell by introducing the actual reason everyone is in the room. So the warm-up runs ten minutes longer than it needs to, and the buyer starts to wonder if the rep is going to get to the point or whether something is wrong.

The transition is the closer's call. Getting it wrong on either side is the most common rookie failure I see, and it has nothing to do with the script.

It has to do with reading the room.

How the Warm-Up Changes by Quadrant

The warm-up principle is universal. The *time horizon* is not.

- In **Quadrant 1**—small dollar, transactional—the warm-up is seconds. A retail clerk who makes eye contact, uses the buyer's name, and says one specific thing has done the whole warm-up. "Love that watch. Vintage?" Three seconds. Trust earned. The sale can happen in the next minute.
- In **Quadrant 2**—large dollar, transactional—the warm-up is the chapter you've just read. Three to ten minutes. The whole arc of the Charlotte family at the practice area. This is the warm-up most reps are trained on, even when they don't work in this quadrant.
- In **Quadrant 3**—small dollar, complex—the warm-up is the entire first meeting. The pitch may not come up at all. The first meeting is for trust, education, and stakeholder mapping. The pitch arrives at meeting two or three.
- In **Quadrant 4**—large dollar, complex—the warm-up is the first meeting and possibly the second. The pitch may not arrive until meeting three. The mortgage originator who sits down with a first-time buyer and starts pitching the loan at minute fifteen will lose the buyer to a competitor who took three meetings to earn the same conversation.

The principle is the same in all four quadrants. The work of the warm-up—surfacing the buyer's interests, demonstrating that the rep sees them, establishing trust—doesn't change.

What changes is the clock.

The salesperson who runs a Quadrant 2 warm-up timeline on a Quadrant 4 deal will close nothing, because the buyer needs more time than the rep has allocated. The salesperson who runs a Quadrant 4 warm-up timeline on a Quadrant 2 deal will close nothing either, because the decision window will dissolve before the warm-up is even finished.

This is the chapter's most important callback to the framework. The warm-up is a quadrant-aware move, even though the principle is universal.

What the Rookies Get Wrong

There are four common failures.

Skipping the Warm-Up to Save Time

New reps believe that the warm-up is friction before the real work begins. They try to compress it, get through it, move on to the pitch where they think the selling actually happens. The buyers feel the rush and close down before the pitch lands. The reps who take this approach consistently underperform their peers by significant margins for reasons they can't explain.

The warm-up isn't friction. It's the foundation. The deals close faster when the warm-up is full than when it's shortened.

Asking Warm-Up Questions Without Listening to the Answers

The script teaches the questions. But the script doesn't teach that the *answers* are the deal's intelligence file. Many reps collect the answers as if they were ticking boxes—*Kids: two. Vacations: mostly beach. Work: accountant.*—and then never use any of it again. The buyer notices. The whole warm-up reads as performative because, in fact, it was. And information collected but never used is the same as information never collected—except worse, because the buyer told you what mattered and watched you ignore it.

The veteran's warm-up is also a working notebook. Every detail surfaced in the first five minutes is in play for the entire ninety. The son's golf came up in the first three minutes. It was still in play at the close.

Returning to the Warm-Up Topics with Manufactured Curiosity

"So tell me more about your kids" twenty minutes after the kids first came up reads as performative if it isn't grounded in something the buyer actually said. The buyer will sense the difference between an organic follow-up and a manufactured one. The organic version sounds like "You mentioned earlier that your daughter's into soccer—is she playing year-round?" The manufactured version sounds like "And the kids? Tell me more about the kids."

The veteran builds on what was actually shared. The rookie reaches for it.

Treating the Warm-Up as a Separate Phase Rather Than the Foundation of Every Subsequent Move

This is the worst of the four because it's the hardest to see in your own work.

The rep believes that the warm-up is over once the pitch begins. The warm-up topics get shelved. The rep moves into product mode, then objection-handling mode, then close mode—each one running on its own logic.

The veteran knows that the warm-up never ends. The son's golf is still in the room during the pricing conversation. The wife's hesitation about money is still in the room during the close. The shared Sunday afternoons watching Tiger are still in the room when the contract gets signed, because they are the reason the contract is getting signed.

The warm-up is not a phase. It's the relational ground that every later move stands on.

The reps who understand this close more deals.

The reps who don't, don't.

The Field Drill

Before your next sales conversation, write down three pieces of personal information you intend to know about the buyer by the end of the first five minutes. Not generic—specific. Their kids' names, where they grew up, what they actually do for a living and not just their job title, what they did last weekend, and so on.

Then write down one piece of that information you intend to use again in the closing conversation.

After the meeting, audit yourself honestly.

Did you collect the three? Did you actually use the one?

If you collected fewer than three, the warm-up didn't happen—you were running through it as a formality. If you used none of them later, the warm-up was theater—you collected information you never planned to deploy.

The veterans collect everything and use what matters. The rookies collect generic information and use none of it.

Run this drill for one week. Track it. The numbers will tell you something about your own work that you may not want to know.

The Dawsons signed before they left the resort that day.

The contract included access to golf properties across the country and overseas. Three championship courses on the home property. Practice access at every affiliated resort. Noah was sixteen years old. Vacation ownership for that family wasn't a vacation product; it was a college-prep program with a beach attached.

I've thought about that tour many times in the years since. The deal wasn't closed by the pitch. It wasn't closed by the pricing. And it wasn't closed by the resort's amenity list, even though the amenity list was extraordinary.

It was closed by the moment Hank looked across the practice area at a stranger who had just noticed his son's grip on a borrowed seven-iron, and decided this might be a conversation worth having.

The warm-up is the deal.

Everything else is the paperwork.

Next chapter: The Question Is the Work—why Implication questions still win deals, the four question types every salesperson needs, and the one question that closes more sales than any technique in the canon.

CHAPTER 4
THE QUESTION IS THE WORK

Daniel and Sofia had been on the resort property for three days when they walked into my private cabana for the upgrade presentation.

They were existing owners. Two-bedroom unit. Loved the resort. Came every year. Had brought their kids and were now bringing their grandkids. The kind of owners who renewed without ever wondering whether they should. They were on the floor that afternoon because their account had been flagged for a premium upgrade, and they had agreed—politely, without enthusiasm—to hear what the upgrade looked like.

I had done the warm-up. We had talked about the grandkids by name—Paris was the youngest, just starting to walk. We had talked about the trip Daniel and Sofia had taken to Tuscany the year before, and the trip to Portugal they were considering next year, and the part of their retirement where they wanted to stop renting villas in Europe and start owning the equivalent of one through the resort's international network. The warm-up had been forty-five minutes, and it had been real. They had been engaged. They had asked their own questions about the upgrade. They had told me they were "definitely interested."

And then they had stopped.

You can feel it when a deal stalls. The buyer is still polite. The conversation is still flowing. But the engagement that had been climbing for the last half hour has flattened, and the next decision—the actual decision the room is here to make—is not happening.

I had reached the moment most reps panic at. The script said to start closing. The pricing was on the table. The buyer was responsive but not moving. The rookie's move at this moment is to start pitching harder—to recap the benefits, to surface a new feature, to introduce time pressure that wasn't there before.

Instead, I closed the folder.

I didn't say anything for a few seconds. Sofia was watching me, not Daniel. Daniel was looking at the folder, then at Sofia, then at me.

I waited until they were both looking at me.

Then I asked.

"What's keeping you from saying yes today?"

Daniel started to give the answer he had been preparing. "We're still thinking about it. Big decision."

I didn't respond. I let the silence sit. He waited for me to fill it. I didn't. He glanced at Sofia.

That was when she said it.

"I worry we'd use it twice a year and feel stupid."

Daniel turned to look at her. He hadn't heard her say it before either.

We had been talking about this upgrade for forty-five minutes inside the cabana—and across three days on the property before that. In all that time, Sofia had never named the real thing standing in her way. She named it now, because I asked one question and then stopped talking.

Daniel spoke first. He asked her how often they even used what they already had.

Sofia answered him honestly. A bigger unit meant a bigger commitment, she said. And a bigger commitment was a bigger thing to be wrong about.

That was it. That was the fear. It had been sitting under every conversation for three days, and neither of them had said it out loud until now.

I let them talk. Two, maybe three minutes. I didn't interrupt.

When they stopped, I said one thing.

"That's the real reason right there. Now we can work with it."

What Sofia finally said was the thing that survives the floor. "Still thinking" is noise—you can't do anything with it. But a named fear? A real reason? That, you can work with.

Daniel and Sofia signed the upgrade twenty minutes later.

We didn't solve Sofia's fear by pretending it wasn't there. We solved it by naming it—and then answering it directly. The upgrade was actually built to give them more control over how they used it, not less. More flexibility, not a bigger trap. Once Sofia understood that, she wasn't saying yes to the thing she'd been afraid of. She was saying yes to something she finally understood.

The deal closed because of one question.

I didn't give them new information after I asked it. I didn't pitch harder. I didn't add urgency. I just asked the question and waited for the answer that was already in the room.

This chapter is about that question, and the family of questions it belongs to, and a second family of questions that does a different job, and the rookies' near-universal failure to know that either family exists.

Questions Are the Work

Most reps treat questions as obligation.

The script says to run a discovery phase. The training says to ask open-ended questions. The trainer says to listen for the buyer's pain points and reflect them back. The rep absorbs all of this and runs through it as a checklist exercise on the way to the part of the conversation they actually believe in—the pitch.

This is the central misunderstanding about questioning that the canon has not fully corrected.

The questions are not the discovery phase. The questions are the work.

The pitch is downstream of the questions. The close is downstream of the questions. The buyer who has answered the right questions has done the rep's work for them—they have surfaced their own pain, named their own implication, articulated their own objection, and reached for the rep's hand in the dark of their own decision. The rep's job at that point is to confirm what the buyer has already figured out and offer a structure to act on it.

Reps who understand this close more. Reps who treat questions as throat-clearing close less. The gap between the two groups is enormous, and most of it lives in this single misunderstanding.

In 1988, Neil Rackham published *SPIN Selling*. He had recorded 35,000 sales calls—at the time, the largest empirical study of sales conversations ever conducted—and he found that the highest-performing reps asked more questions than their peers, and *different* questions. Rackham named four question types: Situation, Problem, Implication, and Need-Payoff (hence the acronym SPIN). He argued that great salespeople ran them in sequence and that the implication questions in particular were the difference between mediocre reps and great ones.

Rackham was right.

His framework survives the floor. The four question types he named are real, they map to actual moves that veteran closers run, and the implication questions remain the single most underused tool in modern questioning. Any rep who hasn't read Rackham is rebuilding his work badly from scratch.

But Rackham missed two whole families of questions that have been on every sales floor in the country for as long as anyone can remember. He missed them because he couldn't have seen them. He was studying enterprise B2B sales—Quadrant 4 work in the matrix you met in Chapter 1. The two question families he missed live primarily in the commissioned consumer sales of Quadrant 2, which is the world I came up in—the world that Rackham didn't study.

This chapter takes Rackham at full strength on SPIN. Then it adds what he couldn't see.

The Four Rackham Types

Run through Rackham's framework quickly, because the rest of the chapter assumes it.

Situation Questions

What is the buyer's current state? Where are they coming from? What is the context?

- "How long have you been a member here?"
- "What does your current vacation routine look like?"
- "Tell me about your last big trip."

These are useful. Rackham warned that buyers tire of them fast, and the floor confirms that. Two or three good situation questions, asked during the warm-up rather than as a separate phase, do the work. More than that and the buyer starts wondering why the rep doesn't just check the file.

Problem Questions

What isn't working? What is the pain? What would they fix if they could?

- "What about your current setup has been frustrating?"
- "What does your family wish they had more of?"
- "What about last year's vacation would you change?"

Useful when there's real trust in the room. Premature problem questions—asked before the warm-up has earned the right to dig—read as predatory. The rep is fishing for pain to exploit. The buyer feels it.

Implication Questions

What does that problem cost? What happens if nothing changes? What is the cumulative effect of the current state?

- "What does it cost you to keep renting a different villa every year?"
- "If you keep waiting until the kids are older, how many more summers does that leave?"

- "What is the long-term math if your vacation budget keeps going up at this rate?"

This is the single most underused question type in modern sales. Most reps ask about problems and then immediately jump to solutions. They never ask the buyer to feel the *cost* of the status quo. The buying decision then feels optional, because the status quo hasn't been made expensive enough in the buyer's own mind for the alternative to feel urgent.

Implication questions are how mild interest becomes a real buying decision. Reps who learn to run them outperform reps who do not. This is Rackham's biggest single contribution to the canon, and it remains the most useful technique he named.

Need-Payoff Questions

What would it look like if the problem were solved? What value would that create?

- "If you owned a property like this, what would your travel schedule look like?"
- "If your family had a place that was always theirs, what changes for the kids?"
- "What would it mean to be done renting?"

These tee up the pitch by letting the buyer articulate the value they would receive. Veteran move: Ask the need-payoff question and *do not* immediately deliver the pitch. Let the buyer fill in their own picture. Then the pitch confirms what they've already imagined.

That is the Rackham toolkit. It works. The floor uses it. Reps who run it well do better than reps who don't.

And now we leave Rackham.

Question Family A: Truth Questions

There is a family of questions Rackham never named.

They surface what the buyer is hiding.

Not what they haven't yet said because nobody has asked. This is about what they're actively *not* saying—what they're tucking behind a polite objection, what they haven't even fully named to themselves, what is in the room without being in the room.

I call them truth questions. They do diagnostic work. They're not closes, they're not pitches, and they're not need-payoffs. They surface the real objection so the rest of the conversation can proceed honestly.

There are three versions in regular floor rotation. Each does slightly different work.

The Opener

"What's keeping you from saying yes today?"

This is the version I asked Daniel and Sofia—the most direct of the three. No qualifier, no softener, no escape hatch for the buyer. The rep has named the close, named the resistance, and put both on the table simultaneously.

This version takes the most confidence to deliver. The buyer hears the absence of softening and reads the rep as a peer rather than a vendor. A rep who can ask this question without flinching is signaling that they're not afraid of the answer—and the buyer adjusts.

This should be asked at the moment the buyer is close but not moving. The deal is alive. The information is in the room. The buyer is responsive but stalled. That is the opener's moment.

The Isolator

"Other than affordability, is there anything else keeping you from saying yes today?"

This is used when money has already entered the conversation. The buyer has raised price as a concern. The rep takes that concern seriously—doesn't dismiss it, doesn't negotiate it away—but *separates* it from everything else.

Most buyers use money as a polite stand-in for a different real objection. The buyer says, "It's a bit expensive," the rep spends forty minutes negotiating price, and the deal walks anyway because the actual concern was identity, or the spouse, or fear of being wrong, or a memory of being burned once before.

The isolator gives the buyer permission to say "Actually, money is the whole thing" (in which case, the deal becomes a financing conversation) or "Now that you mention it, there is something else" (in which case, the real conversation begins).

Either answer is useful. The bad outcome is when the rep doesn't ask, negotiates a price that the buyer accepts in the moment and rescinds later, and the deal dies anyway, with everyone's time wasted.

The Soft Isolator

"Other than money, what else would stop you from moving forward?"

This is the gentler cousin of the isolator, with two important craft differences.

"Moving forward" is softer than "saying yes today." It gives the buyer permission to imagine a future commitment rather than a present one. This lowers the temperature of the question when the rep reads that the buyer is on guard.

"What else would stop you" is hypothetical rather than diagnostic. The buyer isn't being asked to confess current resistance—they're being asked to imagine what might stop them. This is a kinder framing and surfaces the same information.

The best time to use this question type is when the buyer is more skittish, when trust is still building, or when the rep needs to soften the close-the-folder energy that the direct opener carries.

The veteran has all three versions and reads the room to pick which one fits.

- High-trust moment, buyer is confident, decision feels close → the opener.
- Money has been raised, buyer needs face-saving room → the isolator.
- Money has been raised, buyer is more guarded, you need to lower the temperature → the soft isolator.

The point isn't to memorize three lines. The point is to understand that a veteran closer has a *family* of diagnostic questions and chooses contextually. The canon teaches single techniques as if they were universal. The floor teaches families of moves with contextual selection.

Daniel and Sofia got the opener because they were existing owners, deeply engaged, and sitting in a high-trust moment where I had earned the right to ask directly. A first-time buyer on a Saturday tour at the cold property would've gotten the soft isolator instead. Same family of questions—different deployment.

Question Family B: Conditional Closes

There is a second family of questions that Rackham never named.

These are not diagnostic. They're commitment-extraction questions. They neutralize one variable—usually money—and ask the buyer to commit to the deal *if* that variable is solved.

The structure: "If we solved X, would you do Y today?"

A diagnostic question asks the buyer what is in their way. A conditional close *removes* a specific obstacle and asks for a contingent yes. They feel similar, but they do completely different work.

There are three versions in floor rotation.

The Structural Close

"If we could structure your ownership comfortably within your budget, would we move forward today?"

This is the most flexible of the three. It doesn't name a specific number or a specific payment. It commits the rep to *structure*, which gives the rep the widest possible latitude to come back with whatever financing solution actually works.

The buyer commits to a solution category rather than to a specific term sheet. The rep then has room to build the structure that meets the commitment.

This is best used when the rep doesn't yet know which financing levers will land—payment, rate, term, down payment, or some combination—and wants the buyer to commit to the *category* of yes before the math is solved.

The Payment Close

"Assuming we can get the payment where it needs to be, are we ready to do this?"

More aggressive. It narrows the variable to a single number—the monthly payment.

This question is used when the rep has read that payment-per-month is the buyer's mental anchor. For most consumer purchases, it is. Buyers in their thirties and forties think in terms of monthly payments because their financial lives are organized in monthly cash flows. Buyers in their sixties and seventies often think in terms of total price because their financial lives are organized around assets.

Read which one your buyer is thinking in, and ask the question that matches.

The Number Close

"What if I told you we could make this work at $X—would we have a deal?"

The most aggressive of the three. The rep names a specific dollar figure and asks for commitment against that figure.

This is best used in two situations. First, when the rep is confident they can get to that number (they're not bluffing—they have the authority and the structure to make it real). Second, when the rep is reading that the buyer is testing whether the rep has authority to negotiate, and the question puts both authority and commitment on the table simultaneously.

This version is the riskiest. If the buyer says yes, the rep had better be able to deliver the number. If the buyer says no, the rep has burned the strongest version of this move and now has to fall back to a softer variant of the same family.

Veterans use it sparingly. Rookies shouldn't use it at all until they've run the other two many times first.

The deal that taught me Family B was with a couple I'll call Brian and Rachel. Different tour, different week.

Brian was a successful contractor. Forty-two years old. Rachel was an interior designer running her own studio. They were on the property because Rachel had wanted to look at vacation ownership for two years, and Brian had finally agreed to a tour to make her stop bringing it up.

He wasn't going to buy. He had told her he wasn't going to buy. She had told me, during the warm-up at the welcome center, that she didn't expect him to buy. It was a tour to satisfy a long-running disagreement, not a tour to close a deal.

The warm-up worked. Brian relaxed. He started asking real questions. By the time we got back to the cabana, he was—to Rachel's surprise—engaged. They were talking to each other about possibilities. The conversation had crossed from compliance into curiosity.

Then we hit the math.

Brian's face changed when the numbers came out. Not unfriendly, just professional. He looked at the figures the way a contractor looks at a bid that doesn't pencil out.

He said, "Look, this is interesting. But the math has to work. We rent a lake house every summer for eight thousand a month. Anything that costs us more than that on a monthly basis is a no for us."

He thought he had ended the conversation. But he hadn't. He had handed me a number.

I did the math on a napkin in front of them. The monthly payment, structured over the term we had been discussing, came to roughly $6200 a month—lower than what they were already spending on the rental.

I slid the napkin to him.

"If the monthly payment is equal to or less than what you're currently paying to rent, are we signing today?"

I didn't pitch. I didn't soften. I asked the question and waited.

Rachel was watching Brian. He was looking at the napkin. The math was the math. There was no honest "no" available to him at the level of the math. He had named the criterion. The criterion was met.

He set the napkin down and looked up at me.

"My father bought a vacation property when I was a kid," he said. "He lost it in the divorce. Lost it twice—first the house, then the peace. My mother still brings it up twenty-three years later. I promised myself I would never be that guy."

Rachel went still. She had been married to him for eleven years and had never heard him say this.

That was the moment the deal was actually alive.

Question Family C: Identity Audits

There's a third family of questions, rarer than the other two. Most reps never deploy it because most reps never get the conversation deep enough to need it.

The conditional close did its job with Brian. It neutralized money and revealed that money was never the real objection. The real objection was identity. Brian was not refusing a vacation ownership purchase because the math didn't work; he was refusing because buying one would mean becoming his father.

This is the level the conversation had been hiding under the polite objection of "the math has to work." And there was no way to surface it without first running the conditional close that removed the polite objection.

What I did next was the third family of questions—the one no canon book has named. I had heard veteran closers run them. I had run them myself only a handful of times across twenty-one years. The opportunity is rare. The move requires that the buyer has just disclosed something identity-level—a fear about who they are, who they might become, who they refuse to be.

You ask them to audit the fear against another part of their own identity.

"Is the fear of repeating your father bigger than the fear of losing your wife's respect for saying no to something she clearly wants?"

I asked Brian exactly that.

I didn't raise my voice. I didn't lean forward. I asked it the way you would ask a doctor whether a diagnosis was serious—with full attention, no theatrics, in a register the buyer couldn't mistake for a closing technique.

Rachel didn't move. Brian looked at her. Then he looked at the napkin. Then he looked at me.

The identity audit works because it puts two parts of the buyer's identity in conflict and asks them to choose. Brian had been organizing his life around being *not his father.* That was a real identity, and a defensible one, and I wasn't telling him that he was wrong to hold it. I was asking him whether it was bigger than another identity he was also organizing his life around—being Rachel's husband. Being the kind of partner who could say yes to something his wife had wanted for two years.

The buyer either resolves the audit by signing—choosing the identity that was about to be violated by saying no—or by walking, owning the identity they had been protecting all along.

Brian signed.

He took eleven minutes to make the decision. I didn't say anything during those eleven minutes. Rachel didn't say anything either. He sat with the question and the math and the room and the marriage, and he chose.

He told me, after the contract was signed, that the question had felt like an X-ray of a thing he had been carrying for twenty-three years and had never let anyone touch.

I told him I was glad he was Rachel's husband.

We shook hands. They drove home that evening with a vacation ownership contract that Rachel had been wanting for two years and a marriage in which a hidden room had just been brought to light.

The identity audit is not a question for every tour.

Most deals never get deep enough to need it. The buyer's real objection is something Family A or Family B can surface and resolve. The identity audit is for the rare moment when the conditional close has surfaced a real objection but a *deeper* one is still underneath—and that deeper one is about who the buyer believes they are.

When you see that moment, you have to ask the audit, or you have to walk away from the deal. There's no middle option. Pretending the buyer's identity-level resistance is not in the room is the same as ending the conversation while pretending it's still happening.

The audit's structure is always the same.

Is your fear of X bigger than your other commitment to Y?

X is the identity the buyer is protecting. Y is the identity the buyer is also trying to live up to. The audit asks which is more important to them.

You don't get to choose for them. You only get to ask.

This is the part of the chapter where I want to be especially careful. The identity audit, used incorrectly, becomes manipulation. It's simply too sharp a tool for casual deployment. A rookie who has just learned it will use it everywhere, and it won't work. The buyer will read the move as a sales tactic dressed up as therapy, and they'll pull back.

The audit works when the conditional close has done its job first and when the buyer has *volunteered* the identity-level objection. Brian didn't just have a hesitation about money. He had told me, unprompted, the story of his father. He had named the identity he was protecting. He had put the audit's first variable on the table himself. All I did was name the second one—his marriage—and ask which was bigger.

If Brian hadn't told me about his father, the audit wouldn't have been available to me. If he had told me about his father in a different register—bitter, defensive, closed—the audit would've been wrong to ask. The opportunity has to be earned by the buyer's own disclosure, and the rep has to read that the disclosure is sincere before deploying the move.

When it works, it works at a level no other question can reach.

When it doesn't work, it never should've been asked.

The Pause

There is one technical skill that runs underneath all six question types—one that most reps never develop.

The pause.

After you ask a real question, you wait. You wait longer than is comfortable. You wait until the buyer fills the silence—and you let them fill it with whatever surfaces, including the answer they didn't expect to give.

The rookie's mistake is rushing to fill the silence themselves. They ask the question, get nervous when the buyer pauses, jump in with a softening clarification or a reformulation, and cost themselves the answer that was about to come.

Sofia's "I worry we'd use it twice a year and feel stupid" came after a silence I let sit for somewhere between four and six seconds. That's a long time in a sales conversation. Most reps can't hold it. They feel the silence as a failure of the question and reach for another move.

The veteran sits in the pause.

Brian's eleven-minute pause before signing—eleven minutes of silence in a room where the salesperson is normally talking—was the longest pause of my career. I sat in it because I knew the question had landed. He needed time to answer it inside himself. Anything I said in those eleven minutes would have been an interruption of work he was doing on his own behalf.

The discipline is small. The skill is large. Every great closer can sit in a five-second silence without flinching. Most rookies can't sit in a two-second one.

Run all six question types you want. But if you can't hold the pause, the questions won't work.

How the Question Families Change by Quadrant

The six question types are universal. But their pacing and weight change by quadrant.

- **Quadrant 1—Small, Transactional:** Questions are light, fast, often nonverbal. The retail clerk who reads the buyer's posture and asks one well-placed question has done the work. The full taxonomy is rarely needed.
- **Quadrant 2—Large, Transactional:** The whole toolkit: SPIN, plus truth questions, plus conditional closes, plus the rare identity audit. The tour-line work of this chapter. This is where the questioning craft is most developed and where the floor tradition is richest.
- **Quadrant 3—Small, Complex:** Questions stretched across multiple meetings. You earn the right to ask harder questions in meeting two by demonstrating that you absorbed the

answers from meeting one. The identity audit, if it appears at all, comes very late in the relationship.

- **Quadrant 4—Large, Complex:** Questions are the entire first meeting, possibly the first two. The pitch arrives only after the buyer has been thoroughly questioned and feels seen. The mortgage originator who sits down with a first-time buyer and starts pitching the loan at minute fifteen will lose the buyer to a competitor who took three meetings to earn the same conversation.

The taxonomy travels. The clock changes.

What the Rookies Get Wrong

Four common failures:

- **Treating Questions as a Phase Rather Than the Work:** Reps think they're *in discovery* for the first ten minutes and then they're *in pitch.* The veteran knows there's no phase change. Questions run throughout, including after the pitch begins. The buyer who's being questioned the entire conversation feels seen the entire conversation. The buyer who's being questioned only at the start feels like the warm-up was theater.
- **Skipping Implication Questions:** The single most common rookie failure. Reps ask about problems and then immediately jump to solutions. They never ask what the problem *costs.* Without that step, the buyer doesn't feel the weight of the status quo, and the buying decision feels optional. Implication questions are the difference between a buyer who's *interested* and a buyer who's *moving.*
- **Asking Softening Questions Instead of Real Ones:** "Do you mind if I ask . . . ?" / "Is it okay if we talk about . . . ?" / "This may be a stupid question, but . . ." These are throat-clearing. They train the buyer to brace for something the rep is afraid to ask. The veteran asks the question directly, in a level voice, and lets it land. Real questions don't need permission.

- **Filling the Pause:** Already covered above, but worth naming as a rookie failure. The rep who can't sit in the pause is the rep who never gets the real answer. Every great closer can sit in a five-second silence without flinching. Most rookies can't sit in a two-second one.

Before the field drill, one confession.

Both deals in this chapter closed, but many of mine did not. The question families don't guarantee a sale. They guarantee that if the deal is alive, you will find out what's keeping it that way—and they will give you a clean no when the deal was never alive in the first place. A clean no is sometimes the gift of the chapter. The deals that walked, and the cost of a career of walks, are the subject of a later chapter in this book. The point of this one is the questions themselves, used in the deals that lived.

The Field Drill

In your next sales conversation, count three things:

- The number of real questions you asked. Not softening questions. Not procedural questions. Real ones—situation, problem, implication, need-payoff, truth, conditional, or audit. Count them.
- The number of times you let the buyer fill a silence without you breaking it. Not just pauses. *Silences.* Moments where you finished asking and waited for whatever came next, regardless of how long it took.
- Whether you asked a truth question or a conditional close at the close.

After the meeting, audit yourself honestly:

- If you asked fewer than ten real questions in an hour-long conversation, you were pitching, not questioning.

- If you let the buyer fill silence fewer than five times, you were running the conversation instead of conducting it.
- If you didn't ask either a truth question or a conditional close, you didn't run the chapter.

Run this drill for one week. Track the numbers. They will tell you something about your own work that you may not have known you needed to see.

Daniel and Sofia signed because Sofia named her fear and we worked with it instead of around it.

Brian and Rachel signed because Brian named his father and the audit asked him to choose which of his identities he was actually trying to live up to.

Neither deal closed because of a pitch.

Both closed because of a question.

The veteran asks. The rookie tells. That is the whole difference.

Next chapter: Reading the Table—how to identify the silent decision-maker, the partner who hasn't spoken, and the blocker who will kill the deal at the table if you don't read them first.

CHAPTER 5
READING THE TABLE

The conference room smelled like stale coffee and new carpet.

Mario sat forward, elbows on the table, already nodding before I finished the sentence. Maria sat back, arms crossed, her wedding ring catching the fluorescent light as she turned it around her finger for the third time.

I had been a licensed mortgage originator for about five years by then. I knew within the first ninety seconds that Mario would sign anything I put in front of him. I also knew that Maria had not said a word—not hello, not yes, not even a head nod—since they sat down.

The closing disclosure was on the table. Final numbers. A thirty-year fixed. A monthly payment of $2,847.

Mario looked over at her. "That's actually lower than we thought. Right, babe?"

She didn't look back at him.

Then she spoke for the first time. Not to me. Not to Mario. To the window.

"We should have my dad look at this."

Mario started to push back. "Honey, we've been over it. Dave already—"

She cut him off. "He's an accountant. Retired. He's done this for forty years."

She pulled out her phone. Checked the time. Didn't put the phone down.

That was the signal.

The absent stakeholder—Maria's father—was in the room. Maria was already consulting him in her head. The closing disclosure on the table was not the document she was reading. She was reading some version of it that her father had not yet annotated, and she wasn't going to sign until he had.

This chapter is about the person in the room who isn't talking, and the person *not* in the room whose voice is in the room anyway.

It's about how to read the table you're actually sitting at, which is almost never the table you think you're sitting at.

The Buyer Doing the Talking Is Rarely the Decision-Maker

Most reps default to the most engaged person in the room.

They do it because it's easy. The engaged person is leaning in. The engaged person is using your name. The engaged person is asking questions that signal interest. Every social instinct trained into us from childhood says to address the person who's engaging with you, and most reps follow that instinct without ever questioning it.

But that instinct is wrong.

The engaged person is usually the advocate. The advocate already wants to buy. The advocate scheduled the appointment, or pushed for the tour, or talked their partner into the meeting in the first place. The advocate doesn't need to be sold. The advocate has been doing the selling on your behalf, inside the household, for weeks before they ever walked into the room.

The skeptic is the deal.

The skeptic is the one watching, not talking. The skeptic is the one who came along, who agreed to be in the room, who has reserved judgment, and who holds the veto. The skeptic is usually quieter—sometimes silent for the entire meeting. They're paying close attention, but they're paying attention to *you*, not to the product. They're deciding whether you can be trusted before they decide whether your offering can be.

If you address the conversation to the advocate, you confirm a yes that was already in the bank, and you lose the only person in the room whose vote mattered.

The canon hasn't named this clearly. Carnegie wrote about rapport in general—be interested in people, remember names, listen—but he didn't distinguish between the advocate and the skeptic. Dixon and Adamson, in *The Challenger Sale*, introduced the *Mobilizer* concept, but the Mobilizer is the advocate inside the buyer organization, not the silent stakeholder seated across the same table. Voss came closest in *Never Split the Difference*, but he was writing about adversarial negotiations where the harder counterparty is the entire other side, not a quiet partner sitting next to the easier counterparty on the same team.

The floor has known about the silent stakeholder for as long as there have been sales floors. The books just haven't caught up yet. This chapter is the practitioner's correction.

Reading the Table

I want to be honest about something before going further.

Regarding the diagnostic moves I'm about to name—the glance, the phone, the name test, the body geometry—I didn't run them as a conscious checklist in the first meeting with Mario and Maria. I read the room in real time the way veterans read rooms, which is to say I felt it before I could have explained it. The naming came later, when younger originators in our office started asking me how I had known.

What follows is the framework I built in retrospect. It's true. It describes what working salespeople actually do. But the work happened first, and the language came after. That's how most floor craft is acquired: You feel it for a thousand hours, and then one day, you find words for what you've been doing.

With that said, here is what the table told me about Mario and Maria.

- **The Glance:** Every time I asked a question, Mario looked at Maria before he answered. Not always overtly—sometimes a quarter-second flick of the eyes, sometimes a longer check-in. The direction of the glance tells you the hierarchy. The talker who looks at the silent partner before answering is, in his own head, deferring. Maria was the real decision-maker, not Mario. He was the spokesman. She was the principal.

- **The Phone:** Maria checked her phone six times in the first forty minutes. She didn't look at messages. She just held it. Sometimes she would tilt the screen toward herself, glance, and put it back face-down on the table. She wasn't bored, and she wasn't avoiding the conversation. She was just mentally somewhere else, and the "somewhere else" was with her father. Every check of the phone was a small unconscious gesture toward the absent stakeholder she was already consulting.
- **The Name Test:** Mario used my name six times in the first ten minutes. "Dave, can you explain that again?" "That's a great point, Dave." Maria never used my name. Not once. Not even when she finally spoke. The buyer who uses the rep's name is signaling that they have accepted the rep as a peer in the conversation. The buyer who refuses to use the rep's name is signaling that the peer relationship hasn't been earned yet. Maria hadn't granted me admission to the conversation yet. Mario had.
- **The Body Geometry:** Maria's body was closed—arms crossed, legs crossed, angled slightly away from the table. Mario's was open—leaning in, hands on the table, smiling. When Mario opened up further, Maria closed down further. The room had two simultaneous conversations happening, and only one of them was the one being spoken aloud.

I added these signals up and arrived at a quick, accurate read. Maria was the deal. Maria's father was in the room. Mario was a friendly observer of a decision he wasn't the one making.

The rookie's move in this situation is to ask Maria directly what she thinks.

I didn't do that.

The Move I Didn't Make

The rookie's instinct, when the silent partner has been silent too long, is to address them directly. "Maria, what do you think?"

This rarely works. Three reasons.

It puts the silent partner on the spot. They've been silent because they haven't yet decided what they think, or because they *have* decided but aren't ready to say it out loud, or because they don't yet trust the rep enough to share their honest read. A direct question forces them to perform an answer before they're ready, and the answer they give will be a defensive nonanswer. "I don't know. I'm just listening. We need to talk about it." The rep takes the nonanswer at face value, and the conversation continues without the silent partner ever having entered it.

It sidelines the advocate. The advocate has been doing the work of engaging with the rep on behalf of the household. Asking the silent partner directly, in a way that says the advocate's answers don't count, makes the advocate feel reduced to a translator. The advocate gets quiet, the silent partner gets defensive, and the rep has just lost both.

It also signals that the rep is uncertain. A confident rep doesn't need to interrogate the room to find the deal. A confident rep finds the deal by reading the room and addressing it without announcing what they're doing. The direct question signals that the rep has noticed the silent partner is the deal and that they need the silent partner's help to close. The silent partner reads the signal and pulls back further.

The veteran's move is different. The veteran addresses the silent partner without asking them to perform. They bring the silent partner into the conversation by *naming the truth about the room* and giving the silent partner room to enter on their own terms.

Here's what I did with Maria, near the end of the first meeting:

I didn't look at her. I looked at Mario. And I said this:

"Mario, I want to make sure we're not moving too fast. Maria, you're probably running a different set of numbers than Mario is—and I'm going to guess your dad is too. That's actually smart. Most people don't. So here's what I'm going to do. I'm going to send you both a one-page summary. On that page, I'll include the three numbers your dad would likely ask for. Debt-to-income. Cash-to-close breakdown. And the break-even year if you refinance in five years. That way, when you talk to him, you're not guessing."

Three things happened in that paragraph that the chapter wants you to see.

I called Maria by name. I addressed her as a separate analytical entity from Mario: "Maria, you're probably running a different set of numbers than Mario is." She was no longer the spouse who came along. She was the second buyer at the table, with her own set of questions, and I was treating her as a peer rather than as an extension of her husband.

I named the absent stakeholder: "your dad." I hadn't been told the father existed by anyone yet—Maria had only mentioned him in passing once, when she said "He's an accountant" without identifying him as her father. I had inferred his presence in the room, and I had named him. By naming him, I had moved him from a silent veto to a visible participant. He was now part of the conversation rather than a ghost waiting to kill the deal in private.

I respected him before he respected me: "That's actually smart. Most people don't." I had treated the father's expertise as a feature of the conversation rather than a threat to it. The buyer who feels that their absent adviser is being respected by the rep is the buyer who relaxes around the absent adviser. Maria's father hadn't been dismissed. He had been welcomed.

Then I had given Maria something specific to take back to him. The one-page summary. Three numbers her father would actually ask for. The ammunition for her to advocate for the deal in the absent-stakeholder conversation that was going to happen later that night at her father's kitchen table.

That last part was the move most reps never make.

Most reps treat "I need to talk to my dad" as a stall. They try to overcome it. "What if we could lock in this rate today? What if we could give you a small credit if you sign by Friday?" The rookie thinks the absent stakeholder is the obstacle and tries to remove them.

The veteran knows the absent stakeholder is real, has veto power, and is going to be consulted regardless of what the rep says in the room. The veteran's move is not to remove the absent stakeholder. It's to arm the buyer with the specific information the absent stakeholder will need to bless the deal.

Maria looked up.

Not at Mario. At me. For the first time since the meeting started.

She said, "He'll want to see the origination fees line by line."

"Good," I replied. "I'll highlight them. Anything else he'd flag?"

"Prepaids. Escrow. He hates when they pad escrow."

"Got it. I'll show you exactly how we calculated escrow. If your dad still thinks it's high, he can call me directly. I'd actually enjoy that conversation."

She almost smiled.

Not quite. But almost.

I sent the one-page summary that night.

The Second Meeting

Three days later, they came back. Maria was carrying a yellow legal pad with seven questions written on it in her own handwriting. She sat in the same chair. Her arms were still crossed.

But her legs were uncrossed.

A small shift. The kind of shift the rookie misses entirely. The body was no longer at right angles to the table. Maria was forty-five degrees toward the conversation instead of perpendicular to it. The veteran reads that as the silent partner having decided, at home, that this meeting was at least worth attending honestly. She hadn't committed. But she had advanced.

Mario was quieter. He had been coached at home. He was here to support her now. His role had been inverted between meetings.

Before we started on her questions, I told a story.

"Before we get into your list—I had a couple in here last month. Same situation. Wife was quiet for the whole first meeting. Her father was a retired CFO. She asked seventeen questions across three meetings. By the end of the second one, she was the one who said 'let's do this' before her husband did. Not because the numbers changed, but because she realized we weren't trying to hide anything. That's my only goal here. Full transparency."

That was a story aimed directly at Maria. Third-party social proof, in the language of someone like her. A wife who started silent and ended up being the one who closed. A father in the absent-stakeholder seat who hadn't been the deal-killer. A second meeting that ended in a yes.

Maria didn't smile this time. But she nodded. Once. Small nod.

Then we went through her seven questions. I didn't rush. Each question got a number, a document, or an honest "I don't know, but I'll find out." I didn't overexplain. I didn't try to anticipate the questions before they came. I let her ask. I answered. We moved to the next one.

At question five, the shift happened.

She leaned forward. Not a half-lean. A full one. Her arms came uncrossed. She picked up the pen she had been ignoring on the table.

She interrupted me mid-sentence. "Wait. You said the rate lock expires in forty-five days. What happens if we don't close by then?"

The rookie's move at this moment is to keep going at the rep's pace. To finish the sentence that was being interrupted. To answer the new question in the same register as the old one. But that's the wrong move.

The veteran slows down. Matches her pace. Speaks slightly more softly, slightly more carefully. The silent partner has just entered the conversation. The room's center of gravity is now where she is. The rep's job for the next several minutes is to confirm to the room that the silent partner is now the principal interlocutor.

I slowed down. I said, "That's a great question. If we miss the lock, the rate could go up. But we have a buffer. I've already built in fifteen extra days. We're closing on day thirty. You'd have to delay twice to hit the lock expiration. That almost never happens. But if it did, *we* would eat the extension fee, not you. That's in the lender credit section, page four. I'll show you."

I turned the page. Pointed. She read. She read carefully. She didn't look at Mario. He had become the observer now. He was no longer the talker. The room had a new center of gravity, and it was sitting where Maria sat.

She asked the rest of her questions in the same posture. Leaned in. Pen in hand. Engaging directly with me.

When she had finished all seven, there was a small silence at the table. The room was on the edge of a decision, and everyone knew it.

I didn't fill the silence with a pitch.

I looked at her—not at Mario—and asked one question.

"Maria, you've been carrying the weight of this conversation since you walked in. What's been going through your mind that we haven't talked about yet?"

This was the direct invitation. The one that doesn't work when asked too early, because the silent partner isn't ready to surface what they're holding. The one that works at exactly this moment, because the silent partner has been brought forward, the room has shifted toward them, the trust has been earned over two meetings, and the question now lands as an opening rather than as pressure.

She looked at her hands. Then at Mario. Then back at me.

"My dad thinks we're rushing," she finally answered. "He says first-time buyers always overpay. He says we should rent one more year and let rates come down."

I didn't defend.

"Those are all fair," I said. "And he's not wrong—first-time buyers do overpay. Not because they're stupid. Because they fall in love with the house before they fall in love with the math. So let me ask you. Did he see the math? The actual math, not the marketing version?"

"He saw it. He said your numbers were clean."

"Then what's his real concern?"

She paused for a long moment. She looked at Mario. Then at the table.

Then she said it.

"He's afraid we'll get divorced. Like his sister did. And then the house will become a weapon."

The room went still.

Mario reached for Maria's hand across the table. She let him take it.

I waited a few seconds.

Then I said, "Okay. That's not a math problem. That's a marriage problem. And I can't solve that for you. But I can tell you this. Every house you buy is a bet on yourselves. If you're not ready to make that bet, don't sign. Wait a year. No shame in that. But if you *are* ready, then your dad's fear is his, not yours. And you get to choose which one you carry into this closing."

There was a longer silence after that.

Maria didn't look at Mario this time. She looked at me.

"You asked what was going through my mind," she said. "No one had ever asked me that before. Everyone just talks to Mario."

Mario didn't say anything.

He was looking at her, and he didn't interrupt, didn't defend, didn't explain. He sat with the line, and he let it be true in the room without trying to manage it.

She turned the page on the closing disclosure.

She signed.

Mario signed after her.

The deal closed in the room, the same afternoon, before anyone left the table.

What the Rookies Get Wrong

Four common failures, named for the readers who will recognize themselves in them:

- **Defaulting to the Talker:** The rookie addresses the most engaged person in the room because that person is easiest to address. The advocate gets confirmed. The silent partner gets ignored. The deal walks because the silent partner was never persuaded. The fix is to identify the silent partner within the first five minutes and to design the rest of the conversation for them, even when the talker is the one filling the air.
- **Forcing the Silent Partner to Perform:** "What do you think, ma'am?" asked too early, asked too directly, asked in a tone that signals that the rep needs an answer. The silent partner gives a defensive nonanswer. The rep takes the nonanswer at face value. The deal dies. The fix is to address the silent partner by naming the truth about the room—"I'm going to guess you're running a different set of numbers"—rather than by interrogating them.
- **Misreading Silence as Agreement:** The silent partner who isn't speaking is not necessarily agreeing. Most often, they're watching, evaluating, and reserving judgment. The rep who treats silence as a yes is the rep who hears the rescission call on Monday morning. The fix is to read silence as data—what

kind of silence, with what body geometry, with what micro-shifts—and to treat the silent partner's eventual conversion, not the talker's enthusiasm, as the actual signal that the deal is closing.

- **Treating the Absent Stakeholder as a Stalling Tactic:** "I need to talk to my husband before deciding." "I want to run this by my accountant." "My dad has been doing this for forty years." The rookie hears these sentences as polite stalls and tries to overcome them. The veteran hears them as the truth—the absent stakeholder is real, has veto power, and is going to be consulted. The veteran's move is not to remove the absent stakeholder. It's to arm the buyer with the specific information the absent stakeholder will need to bless the deal. This is one of the most powerful moves in commercial selling, and almost no rep makes it.

How Reading the Table Changes by Quadrant

The four signals are universal. The complexity of the table changes by quadrant.

- **Quadrant 1—Small, Transactional:** You are usually reading one buyer. The signals are present but compressed. The retail clerk reads the buyer's body geometry in the first three seconds and adjusts.
- **Quadrant 2—Large, Transactional:** Two to four people in the room, usually a family. The chapter's classic territory for timeshare and high-end retail. The silent partner is almost always present and almost always the deal.
- **Quadrant 3—Small, Complex:** Stakeholders span meetings. The first meeting may have two people in the room; the second may have four; the third may have a stakeholder you've never met. Reading the table becomes *reading who keeps showing up* as the deal progresses, and who has been quietly added to the conversation between meetings.

- **Quadrant 4—Large, Complex:** This is the chapter's natural home. The silent stakeholders may include people you never meet. The accountant. The trust attorney. The aging parent. The business partner. The estranged adult child whose opinion the buyer is anticipating without ever naming. Maria's father is the archetype. He was never in the conference room, and he was the most important person at the table. The veteran knows that the table extends beyond the people sitting at it, and they design the conversation accordingly.

Before the Field Drill

One last note for honesty, before we go.

Mario and Maria signed. Many of my buyers did not. Some deals had silent partners that I read wrong. Some had absent stakeholders I never identified until it was too late. Some had skeptics who were never going to be persuaded by anyone, and the right outcome was a clean walk that I couldn't see coming.

The framework in this chapter is not a guarantee. It's a way to read the room more accurately than the rookie does. The buyer is still the buyer. The veto is still the veto. The relationships at the table are what they are, and you can't change them. You can only see them more clearly and design your work around them.

A clean walk, again, is sometimes the gift of the chapter. The silent partner who declines because the deal is genuinely wrong for their household has done you a favor. They have prevented a rescission, protected the marriage, and preserved your reputation. The walks that come from misreading the table are the ones to grieve. The walks that come from reading the table correctly and respecting what you read are the ones to be proud of.

The cost of a career of walks—and what it takes to survive that cost—is the subject of a later chapter.

The Field Drill

In your next sales conversation, do three things within the first five minutes:

- **Identify the Advocate:** The person leaning in. The person using your name. The person already wanting what you're offering.
- **Identify the Silent Stakeholder:** The person not yet committing. The body geometry that's closed. The phone that stays in the hand. The eyes that flick to the partner before answering. The name that hasn't been used.
- **Identify the Absent Stakeholder:** The father, the accountant, the adult child, the business partner whose opinion is being consulted by the silent partner inside their own head, even though that person is nowhere in the room.

Then, before you make any major move, ask yourself: "Am I designing this conversation for the talker or for the deal?"

After the meeting, audit yourself honestly.

- Did you identify the silent stakeholder correctly?
- Did you address them by name, in passing, with new information, at least three times—without ever putting them on the spot?
- Did you name the absent stakeholder rather than try to overcome them?
- Did you give the buyer something specific to take back to the absent stakeholder?

If the answers are yes, and the deal still walked, the walk was honest. If the answers are no, the walk was avoidable, and this chapter is where you start.

The talker brought Mario and Maria to the table.

The silent partner decided whether they left with a deal.

The absent stakeholder was in the room the whole time, and the deal closed because I named him out loud and respected him.

The advocate isn't the deal. The skeptic is.

Address them.

Next chapter: The Story That Sells—why facts don't move people, the four-part structure of a closing story, and the line between selling and bullshitting.

CHAPTER 6
THE STORY THAT SELLS

Frank walked up to me with his shoulders down.

He had just spent an hour in the cabana with a husband and wife who had come to the resort for a long weekend with their kids. The family was thinking about a second home, or maybe vacation ownership, or maybe neither. They had been polite the whole tour. They had asked some questions. They had said the right things. And then they had given Frank the standard exit line—"We'll think about it, we have a lot to talk about, we appreciate your time"—and Frank had read that line the way most reps read it.

As the end.

He came over to me at the closer's desk. He had the prospect card in his hand and the half-folded body language of a rep who has decided the deal is dead.

He said, "Dave, I have nothing. They're not interested. I'm going to sign them out."

I looked at him for a long moment before I answered.

Twenty-one years on the floor will teach you what "I have nothing" sounds like in the mouth of a rep who has actually run the playbook versus what it sounds like in the mouth of a rep who's about to walk away from a deal that was actually alive.

This was the second kind.

I said, "Frank, you spent an hour with that family. You ate breakfast together. You walked the property together. The kids liked the pool. The wife liked the unit. Tell me you didn't find a single thing to build on in that hour."

He looked at me.

"You did find things," I continued. "You just don't know what to do with them. Bring *me* to the table. Transfer it the way I'm about to tell you to."

I gave him three lines. Word for word.

I told him, "Walk me in. Stand next to me. Don't sit. Don't introduce me as the closer. Don't introduce me as your manager. Introduce me as Dave. Then say this exact sentence."

The sentence I gave him was this:

"Dave, this family and I enjoyed breakfast together, and they commented on how much they love this property. They had a great time. They want to come back. I presented the numbers for ownership, and they said it's not affordable and not what they expected today. But I know you have special programs for first-time ownership at our property. Could you please help this family—if any of that inventory is available?"

Frank repeated it back to me twice. The second time, he got it right.

We walked to the cabana.

He delivered the line exactly as I had given it to him. Walter and Diane looked up. They were still polite, but the politeness had cooled. The exit had already been mentally booked. They were five minutes from being in their car.

I introduced myself.

Then I sat down across from them, and I didn't pitch.

I told them a story.

I told them about a family who had been in that same cabana the year before. Husband from Cleveland, wife from a town twenty miles outside of Cleveland, two kids in elementary school. They had also been a no on the math. They had said it the same way Walter and Diane had said it: "It's not affordable. It's not what we expected."

I told Walter and Diane that the Cleveland family had not bought that day.

I told them what the Cleveland family had done instead.

They had gone home and rented a beach condo for the winter, which they spent only a week at because they had already promised the kids a vacation that year. The rental had cost them a small fortune. The next year, they did it again. The third year, they had done it again. By year four, the math had caught up with them, and they had come back to the resort and asked to talk about ownership a second time. They had spent more on three weeks of rented vacations than they would've spent on the down payment of an ownership stake they would have owned for a lifetime.

I told Walter and Diane that the wife had cried at the table when she signed the second time. Not from joy but from the four years she hadn't been an owner. Four winters that her kids would never get back.

Their older boy, Liam, was twelve by the time they finally bought. He was already half out of the house. The years the parents had wanted to give him—the years of arriving at the same beach, the same week, the same room, the same view, the kids growing up inside one place they could call theirs—those years had been spent renting other people's condos in other people's towns. The math was the same. The years were not.

I stopped there.

Diane was looking at her hands.

Walter was looking at me.

He said, "Why are you telling us this?"

"Because I don't want you to be that family," I replied. "I would rather you walk out of here today and never come back than have you sign something that hurts your household. But I also don't want you to be sitting in a rental condo in three winters wishing you had asked one more question before you left."

Then I asked the question.

"How much did you spend on vacation last year?"

Walter said a number. I asked him how many years that had been the pattern. He told me. I asked him whether they wanted that pattern to continue. He told me they did. They wanted the kids to grow up coming to the same place. They wanted the grandkids, eventually—Thomas was just a baby then—to come to the same place. They wanted what they had felt in those three days on the property to become a thing the family did every year for the rest of their lives.

I hadn't pitched. They were now selling *themselves* on the product.

This is what people mean when they say "the story does the work."

The Cleveland family was real. I had run that tour. The wife had cried at the table when she signed the second time. I have told that story dozens of times in twenty-one years, and it has closed deals every time it landed in the right room. It landed in the right room with Walter and Diane because the structure of their hesitation was the same as the Cleveland family's, and Walter and Diane recognized themselves in the protagonists of a story that had already played out somewhere else.

Recognition is the close. Everything after recognition is paperwork.

The math came back into the conversation about ninety minutes after I had sat down.

I didn't introduce it. Walter did.

He asked me how the numbers actually worked for first-time owners at the property. I walked him through them honestly. I didn't soften them. The deal was a real deal at a real number, and the number was real money for their household.

I asked them one question at the close.

"If this monthly payment is within your budget, and it's the same amount you would've spent on vacation anyway, and it doesn't take food from the table, are you our new owners?"

The phrase "doesn't take food from the table" is not a phrase I learned from a script. It arrived at a closing table one afternoon in my first few years on the floor. I was sitting across from a family—I can't remember now which family it was exactly—and I had reached the moment when the close had to be asked. Something in the room told me that the deal, even at its fair price, was going to cost the household more than it should. The family wanted it. I wanted to sell it. The math worked on paper. But there was something in the way the wife looked at the husband when I said the monthly payment that told me the deal would still take something away from this household that the household couldn't afford to lose.

So I asked the question I hadn't planned to ask: "If this monthly payment is within your budget, and it doesn't take food from the table, are you our new owners?"

The phrase was mine. It came out of my mouth before I decided to use it. The wife looked at me when I said it, and her shoulders dropped two inches.

They signed.

I have asked some version of that question at the close of every deal I have made for over twenty years. It's the line that tells the family, in five words, that I won't let them sign a deal that hurts them. The deal has to be small enough that it doesn't take food from the table. If it's bigger than that, I'm not closing a deal—I'm hurting a family. And the family will find their way back to the truth eventually, and they will hurt me back—through a rescission, through bad word of mouth, or through the long, quiet kind of damage that erodes a salesperson's reputation across years.

Veterans on every floor I've ever worked have a version of this line, even when they don't use the same words. It's the line that distinguishes the closer from the predator. Joe never said the exact phrase, but he ran the same discipline by another name. So did Rick. The line isn't in the canon. It belongs to the floor.

Walter and Diane looked at each other.

There was a silence at the table. Diane's eyes were the ones I was watching. She had been quieter than Walter for most of the meeting. Her face hadn't relaxed until I had told the Cleveland story. She had been the deal, the way Maria had been the deal in Chapter 5, the way the silent partner is usually the deal.

She looked at Walter for a long second.

Then she nodded once.

Walter reached across the table and shook my hand.

The contract was signed within twenty minutes.

When I walked them out to the parking lot, Diane stopped at the door of the cabana and said something I didn't expect. "Thank you for not making us feel stupid."

I didn't know what to do with that line at the time. I do now. It's the line that tells you the entire chapter's argument was true in the room. Walter and Diane hadn't been *not interested*, the way Frank had reported. They had been *afraid of being made to feel stupid*—afraid of being pressured into a deal that would embarrass them, afraid of being treated as marks rather than as a family making a real decision about a real product.

The story I told hadn't pressured them. And the question at the close hadn't pressured them.

What I had done—and what every veteran closer does without quite knowing how to explain it—was tell them a story about people like them and ask them whether they wanted to keep being those people for another four years.

The recognition was theirs.

The decision was theirs.

The deal was mine.

I walked Frank back to the closer's desk afterward. He had stood in the cabana the whole time the conversation was happening. He had watched me do it. He hadn't said anything during the close itself; he had stayed on his feet behind me and watched.

He looked at me when we got back to the desk.

"How did you know they would buy?" he asked.

"I *didn't* know they would buy," I replied. "I just knew they hadn't said no yet. There's a difference."

He started to argue. I held up my hand.

"Frank," I said. "After spending an hour with a family—eating breakfast with them, walking the property with them, watching their kids in the pool with them—you don't have 'nothing.' You have an hour of human contact with people who showed up at the resort because some part of them wanted what we sell. Whether they *will* buy today, you cannot know. Whether they *can* buy today, you don't get to decide. *They* get to decide. Your job is to bring me into the room when you've run out of road, not to sign the tour out for them because you decided they were done."

He was quiet for a moment.

I said the line he is probably still telling other reps about, fifteen years later.

I said, "Never prejudge. You gain nothing. Prejudge a customer, and the best you can do is confirm a guess—the worst is you talk yourself out of a sale that was sitting right in front of you."

That is the chapter.

Facts Persuade, Stories Convert

The reason the Cleveland story closed Walter and Diane—and the reason any story closes any buyer—is not mysterious. It's not magic. It's how the human brain has evolved to process new information, and any closer who has spent enough hours on a sales floor has internalized it whether they know they have or not.

The brain remembers narrative and forgets data.

Most readers can recall, in considerable detail, a movie they saw twenty years ago—the plot, several specific scenes, what one character said, what they were wearing. On the other hand, most readers can't recall the specific facts they were given in a corporate training they sat through six weeks ago. Both events took roughly the same amount of time, but one has lasted decades, and the other has already evaporated.

This is not a flaw in the brain. It's the brain working correctly. The brain evolved to retain *narrative* because narrative carries information about what to do in similar situations later. Facts in the abstract carry no such instructions. The brain processes facts as data and discards them. The brain processes stories as templates for behavior and keeps them.

The salesperson who builds his career on product knowledge—on facts, features, specifications, comparisons—is building it on something the buyer won't remember by the time they reach the parking lot. The salesperson who builds his career on stories is building it on something the buyer will carry into their next conversation, and the one after that. Stories are how influence outlives the meeting.

This is what Daniel Pink touched on in *To Sell Is Human* when he wrote about the Pixar pitch—the six-sentence structure that every Pixar film follows and that, Pink argued, every modern salesperson should know. Pink was correct. He was also late. The Pixar structure isn't a marketing trick that Pixar invented. It's the structure of effective human storytelling that the screenwriting teacher Robert McKee had been teaching for forty years before Pink wrote about it, and that working sales floors had been running for at least a century before McKee named it.

Joe was running this structure in 1989. He had never read Pink or McKee. He had been taught it by the closers who came before him, who had been taught by the closers before them. The structure is older than every book that has been written about it. Like we've seen with other volumes in the canon, the books described what was already happening on the floor.

This is the chapter where we make the structure explicit so that the reader can run it on purpose instead of by accident.

The Four-Part Structure

Every story that converts has four beats. Run them all, and the buyer recognizes themselves in the protagonist. Skip one, and the story is an anecdote—short, entertaining, forgettable.

- **Setup:** Who is the protagonist? What is their situation when the story begins? The setup gives the buyer someone to identify with. It's short—two or three sentences. *I had a family in here a year ago. Husband from Cleveland, wife from a town twenty miles outside of Cleveland, two kids in elementary school.*
- **Stakes:** What is at risk? What does the protagonist stand to lose, or fail to gain? Stakes give the story its weight. Without stakes, the story is decoration. *They had also been a no on the math. They had said it the same way Walter and Diane had said it: "It's not affordable. It's not what we expected."*
- **Turn:** The decision or the event that changes the trajectory. The turn is the moment the story pivots from setup-and-stakes into consequence. *They had gone home and rented a beach condo for the winter. It had cost them a small fortune. The next year, they did it again. The third year, they had done it again. By year*

four, the math had caught up with them, and they had come back to the resort and asked to talk about ownership.

- **Resolution:** What changed for the protagonist as a result? Not what they bought, exactly—what *changed*. The resolution closes the loop and leaves the lesson in the buyer's head without the rep needing to state it. *The wife cried at the table when she signed the second time. Not from joy but from the four years she would never get back. The kids were ten and twelve. They were already half out of the house. The years the parents had wanted to give them had been spent renting other people's condos in other people's towns.*

Notice what is not in any of those four beats.

There is no pitch. There is no product feature. There is no closing line. There is no instruction to the buyer about what they should do. The story has done the entire job of persuasion by *showing* the buyer a version of themselves who waited too long. The buyer's brain does the rest.

When the story is over, the buyer is in a different cognitive state than when it began. They have just lived, vicariously, four years of the wrong choice. They have just felt, briefly, the regret of the wife in the story crying at the table. Their resistance to the deal in front of them has not been argued against—it has been *aged*. The deal looks different now than it did before the story.

This is what people mean when they say "the story does the work."

The rep who learns to tell four-beat stories closes more deals than the rep who has the better script. The rep who never learns it works twice as hard for half the result and never quite figures out why.

The Three Stories Every Salesperson Tells

There are three categories of story that every working salesperson tells, whether they know they're doing it or not. Naming the three categories is the move that turns unconscious craft into conscious technique.

- **The Story About Yourself:** Why are you doing this work? What brought you to this room? What do you believe about what you are selling? This story is small, told briefly, told once.

The buyer needs to know who you are before they can trust what you're saying. The veteran tells this story in ninety seconds and never returns to it. The rookie tells it for ten minutes and bores the room.

- **The Story About the Product:** Not the features—the product's *story.* Why does the product exist? What was it built to solve? Who made it and why? This story positions the product as a response to a real human need rather than as an inventory item to be moved. The veteran tells this story when the buyer asks about the product. The rookie recites the brochure.
- **The Story About *Them*:** This is the most powerful of the three and the one that most rookies never learn. The story is told as if it were about someone else—"I had a family in here last year"—but the story is actually about the buyer in front of you. The buyer recognizes themselves in the protagonist. The recognition is the conversion.

The Cleveland story is a story about Walter and Diane.

Yes, it's told about a different family, in the past tense, and without ever explicitly referencing Walter and Diane's situation. But every detail in it has been selected to mirror something Walter and Diane have either said out loud or shown in their body language during the prior hour. The hesitation on the math. The polite exit line. The kids' ages. The husband running the conversation while the wife sat with her hands in her lap.

Walter and Diane heard the Cleveland story as a story about another family, but their brains processed it as a story about themselves. The gap between those two experiences—the conscious one and the subconscious one—is where the conversion happens.

The veteran picks the story to fit the buyer.

The rookie picks the story to fit the script.

That is the entire difference between Frank declaring "I have nothing" after an hour with Walter and Diane, and me sitting down at the same table and closing the deal inside of two hours by telling them about a family they had never met.

The Line Between Selling and Bullshitting

I want to be careful here.

A serious reader, finishing the section above, may have started to wonder whether storytelling in sales is just sophisticated manipulation. The buyer is being moved by something they think is about someone else when it's actually about them. The rep has selected the story precisely to produce a result. Isn't this just well-engineered persuasion that the buyer can't detect?

The honest answer is that it depends entirely on whether the story is true.

The Cleveland family is real. I ran that tour. The wife really did cry at the table when she signed the second time, four years after the first tour. I have used the story for dozens of years because it's one of the truest examples I've ever seen of what waiting too long actually costs a family.

A true story shared honestly between two adults is an act of mutual recognition. *I'm telling you about another human like you because I think you are like them. I think the years they lost might be years that you're about to lose. I'm giving you that story because it might save you the same regret.* The buyer who hears a true story feels seen. The rep who tells true stories builds a long-term reputation that compounds across a career.

A fabricated story is something else entirely. It's a lie engineered to produce an outcome. The buyer's instinct can almost always tell the difference, even when they can't say what is off. The detail that doesn't quite fit (or seems to fit too perfectly). The protagonist whose life feels generic. The resolution that's too clean. The buyer's brain is exquisitely tuned to detect storytelling that has been manufactured rather than remembered, and the buyer pulls back from a fabricated story the same way they'd pull back from any other dishonest move.

Now, there are gray zones that this chapter can't pretend away. A story that happened, told to a buyer it doesn't perfectly apply to. A story whose details have been slightly sharpened in the retelling. A story being told for the fortieth time, with the previous tellings having tightened the structure beyond what actually happened in the first version. These are real ethical questions, and any working veteran has lived inside them.

My honest stance is to stay as close to true as possible. Every drift toward fabrication is a small withdrawal from a long-term account you are building. Some withdrawals are unavoidable; veterans know they happen and try to keep them small. The salesperson who pretends they've never drifted is lying to themselves first and to their buyers second.

The deeper point is this: The buyer's emotional response to a true story is *data*, not manipulation. The buyer who is moved by the Cleveland story is moved because the Cleveland story matches something real about their own situation. The story has revealed something the buyer was carrying. Honoring that revelation by closing the deal honestly is not manipulation.

Closing the deal *dishonestly*—by telling stories that were never true, or by manipulating a true story to make a buyer sign a deal that's wrong for their household—is.

The line is the truth.

The veteran lives on the right side of it because the floor catches dishonesty within a few quarters. The rookie who hasn't yet learned this is the rookie who washes out by year three.

How Storytelling Changes by Quadrant

The four-part structure is universal. The pacing changes by quadrant.

- **Quadrant 1—Small, Transactional:** Stories are brief and visual. A retail clerk who tells a thirty-second story about another customer who bought the same item has done the work.
- **Quadrant 2—Large, Transactional:** The full four-part structure, told in two to four minutes at the right moment in the conversation. This is the territory of the Cleveland story. Quadrant 2 is where storytelling carries the close more than in any other quadrant, because the buyer has a single decision window, and the story has to do the persuasive work inside that window.

- **Quadrant 3—Small, Complex:** Stories spread across multiple meetings. Each meeting earns a new story. By the third meeting, the buyer has heard four or five stories and is starting to feel they know the rep's whole catalog. The veteran rotates the catalog carefully so that each meeting has a fresh story aimed at the specific question that meeting is meant to address.
- **Quadrant 4—Large, Complex:** Stories are longer, more analytically grounded, and often carry forward through meetings. The Mario and Maria conversation in Chapter 5 used a single story—"I had a couple in here last month. Wife was quiet for the first meeting. Her father was a retired CFO"—and that single story did meaningful work across two meetings. In Quadrant 4, the story has to survive scrutiny across time, so the veteran tends to tell *fewer, more carefully chosen* stories rather than running a high-volume catalog.

The structure travels. The clock changes.

What the Rookies Get Wrong

Four common failures:

- **Telling Stories About Themselves Instead of About the Buyer:** New reps default to autobiography. *Let me tell you about my background. Let me tell you why I love this product.* The buyer hears a story about the rep when they needed a story about themselves. The rep finishes the story feeling they have built rapport. The buyer finishes the story feeling they have just sat through a job interview.
- **Telling Stories Without Stakes:** New reps tell *anecdotes*—short narratives that have a beginning and an end but no real cost to the protagonist. The protagonist didn't stand to lose anything. The buyer hears the anecdote and feels nothing, and the story does no work. The veteran's stories always have stakes. The protagonist had something at risk. The risk is what makes the story matter.

- **Telling the Story and Then Explaining It:** New reps tell a story and then add "and the lesson is . . ." This destroys the story. The buyer's brain was doing the work of recognition. The rep just interrupted that work to deliver the lesson explicitly, which means the buyer no longer has to do the work themselves. The veteran tells the story and stops. The lesson is in the buyer's head. The rep doesn't need to put it there a second time.
- **Reaching for a Story When No Story Is Available:** New reps have a small catalog and reach for stories that don't quite fit the buyer in front of them. The buyer can tell when the story isn't landing. The veteran is willing to *not* tell a story when no story fits. Silence is better than a forced story. The next story in the catalog might fit the next meeting. Save it.

Before the Field Drill

One last honesty.

Walter and Diane closed. Frank's prejudgment was wrong. The Cleveland story has landed in many rooms across many years.

It has also failed in many rooms.

There are buyers who hear the Cleveland story and recognize nothing in it because their situation doesn't match the protagonists'. There are buyers who recognize themselves in the story and still walk because they have decided, honestly, that the deal is not right for their household this year. There are buyers who would have bought regardless of which story they heard, because they had already decided that before they walked in.

The four-part structure doesn't guarantee a close. It guarantees that *if the buyer is alive to the deal*, the story will reach the part of them that decides. The buyers who aren't alive to the deal will walk regardless, and the buyers who were always going to buy will buy regardless of what you tell them.

The storytelling craft doesn't produce results in every room. It produces results in *more rooms* than the rep who tells no stories, and it produces them honestly. It also builds a reputation that compounds.

A clean walk after a well-told story is sometimes the gift of the chapter. The buyer who hears the truth and decides the deal isn't right for them has done the rep a favor that the rep may not recognize until years later.

The deals that walked, and the cost of a career of walks, are still the subject of a later chapter.

The Field Drill

Write down three real stories from your work that have moved a buyer in the past year. Not anecdotes. Stories. With four beats.

For each one, identify:

- The setup. Who was the protagonist? What was their situation?
- The stakes. What did they stand to lose or fail to gain?
- The turn. What decision or event changed the trajectory?
- The resolution. What changed for them as a result?

If you can't identify all four beats clearly, the story is not yet a story. It's an anecdote. Sharpen it. Find the stakes. Find the turn. Make the resolution land.

Then identify which of the three categories each story belongs to—about you, about the product, or about them.

Most reps will find that their catalog is heavily weighted toward stories about themselves and the product. The category most missing—stories about *the buyer*—is the one that closes the most deals. If you can't name three stories from this category, you have just found your homework for the next ninety days.

Frank walked away from a family that wanted to talk.

He had spent an hour with them. He had eaten with them. He had walked the property with them. He had watched their kids in the pool. And then he had stood up from the table, declared they weren't interested, and gone to sign the tour out.

He was wrong about what he had.

I sat down at the same table an hour later, told them one true story, asked one honest question, and closed the deal.

Walter and Diane were not the deal that day.

The deal was the assumption Frank had made when he stood up.

Never prejudge.

You gain nothing.

Next chapter: The Close Is a Moment, Not a Move—why closing technique is the most misunderstood part of the canon, and what veterans actually do in the final ninety seconds of a sale.

CHAPTER 7
THE CLOSE IS A MOMENT, NOT A MOVE

This is the last chapter of Part I.

It is also the shortest, by design. The chapter's argument is that closing is small. It can't make that argument honestly while running long.

What follows is not a new floor anecdote. The book has already given you seven of them. Joe and the family in the Author's Note. Margaret on the balcony. The couple that Margaret's story helped close. The Dawsons. Brian and Rachel. Mario and Maria. Walter and Diane. Seven closes across six chapters.

You have already lived through them once.

This chapter takes you through them again, with only one lens applied: the closing-moment lens. The chapter is the answer to a question the reader may not have known they were carrying through Part I: *When did each of those deals actually close?*

The answer is almost never the moment the contract was signed.

What the Canon Got Half Right

In 1988, Brian Tracy published *The Psychology of Selling*. Tracy was, and remains, the most prolific writer in the closer's tradition. The book—and dozens of others Tracy wrote in the years after—codified the closing playbook that millions of working salespeople were trained on through the eighties, nineties, and early two-thousands. Tracy taught the assumptive close. The alternative close. The Ben Franklin close. The puppy-dog close. The urgency close. The takeaway close. The Columbo close. The catalog runs to dozens of named techniques, each with a script, each with a context.

Tracy was right about one thing and wrong about another, and the canon has been confused for forty years because almost no one separates the two.

Tracy was right about the *asking discipline*. He named, more clearly than anyone else, the rep's responsibility to *ask for the order*. Most reps can't. They run out the clock. They hand the buyer a brochure. They say, "Let me know what you decide," and walk away from deals that were ready to close because they didn't have the spine to ask the question. Tracy diagnosed this failure correctly. The rep who can't ask is the rep who washes out. The floor confirms their diagnosis every day.

But Tracy was wrong about *closing technique*.

The catalog of named techniques is real. Reps have used them for decades. The trainings still teach them. But the techniques are not what's closing the deals. The deals that closed after a technique was applied were already closing, and the technique was just decoration. The deals that walked after a technique was applied were scared off by the technique itself. The catalog is a museum of moves that look like they work but, in the deeper sense, don't actually do the work.

What the veteran actually does at the close is read the moment and ask plainly.

Whether the plain ask uses a phrase the canon would call an *assumptive close* ("How would you like to handle the deposit today?") or a phrase the canon would call a *direct close* ("If this works for you, we have a deal") or no named phrase at all is downstream of one prior thing: Did the rep correctly read that the moment had arrived?

If yes, almost any plain ask will work.

If no, then no technique will save the close.

The technique is not the move. The reading is the move. The asking is the small last step.

The Closing Moment

The closing moment is recognizable. It has signals. The veteran reads them. The rookie misses them or, worse, has been trained to ignore them in favor of running a closing technique on a schedule.

Five signals to name:

- **The Leaned-Back Posture:** Buyers who are still working a decision lean forward. Buyers who have decided lean back. The shift from forward to back is one of the cleanest closing signals available. The buyer has stopped processing and started accepting.
    - Maria leaned forward at question five in Chapter 5. She stayed leaned forward through the rest of the conversation about the rate lock and the closing costs. Somewhere around the divorce-fear revelation, she settled. The posture changed once more—not back into the closed position from the start of the meeting but into a different one entirely. Calm. Decided. The signature came after.

- **The Look Between Partners:** A long, calm look exchanged between two buyers without anything being said is almost always the moment when a household decision has been silently made. The veteran sees the look and waits a beat before asking.
    - Walter and Diane, in Chapter 6, exchanged the look right after the food-from-the-table question. Diane's eyes were the ones I was watching. She nodded once. Walter reached across the table and shook my hand. The conversation between them happened entirely without language. The look was the close.

- **The Volunteered Logistical Question:** "How long does the paperwork take?" / "Can we get started today?" / "When would we need to put a deposit down?" These questions are the buyer pre-living the post-close moment. They have mentally already passed the decision and are now inside the implementation. The deal has closed in their head. The rep's job at this point is to confirm what has already happened.

   - In Chapter 1, after the widow story, the couple began asking questions about the package—how the network worked, what the maintenance fees included, what the booking process looked like. None of those questions are pre-decision questions. They are post-decision questions about a deal the couple had already silently chosen.

- **The Relaxation of Guarded Body Language:** Uncrossed arms. Released shoulders. A small smile. A laugh that wasn't there ten minutes ago. The body has decided before the mouth has said it.
   - The Dawsons relaxed into the tour sometime around the conversation about Noah's grip on a borrowed seven-iron. Hank's posture, Linda's posture, Noah's posture—all three of them entered a different state in the first three minutes. The signature ninety minutes later was not the close. The shift in the practice area was.

- **The Silence After a Substantive Question:** When the buyer goes quiet after asking something serious—not the polite small-talk silence but a longer, more deliberate one—the buyer is processing the deal at full attention. That kind of silence almost never precedes a no. It almost always precedes a yes that hasn't yet been articulated.
   - Brian sat with the identity audit for eleven minutes in Chapter 4. He didn't respond. Rachel didn't respond. The silence was the entire close. The signature was the eleven-minute conversation Brian had with himself, made audible only by his eventual decision to reach for the pen.

Reading any one of these signals is the rep's basic competence. Reading two or three of them at once is the veteran's normal experience of the closing moment.

The rookie either hasn't learned to see them at all, or they've been trained to ignore them in favor of running a closing technique at minute eighty-eight regardless of what the room is doing.

The Seven Closes, Reread

The book has shown you seven closes. Each of them is a case study about the same principle. The signature was the receipt of a decision that had already been made. The closing moment came earlier and was small enough to miss if you weren't watching for it.

- **Joe and the Family in the Author's Note:** Joe told stories until the family recognized themselves in one of them. The close happened in the moment of recognition—somewhere in the third or fourth story, when the husband leaned over to his wife and said something quiet that I couldn't hear from where I was standing. Joe saw the moment. He paused his story. He let the silence sit. Then he asked for the order in a single sentence. The contract was signed inside of three minutes after that. The technique wasn't the close. The story wasn't the close. The recognition was the close.
- **Margaret on the Balcony in Chapter 1:** Margaret had been holding the decision in pieces—the inheritance, the trips her husband had been promising her, the structure of the years she had stopped letting herself live. The close happened when those pieces assembled themselves in her own mind, somewhere during the conversation about what the ownership would force her calendar to do. The signature came later. The decision came when she said *intention* out loud.
- **The Couple That Margaret's Story Closed:** They were quiet for a long moment after I finished telling the story. The husband looked at his wife. She was already looking at him. *That was the close.* They bought a package before they left the property. The actual purchase was paperwork. The decision had happened in the look.
- **The Dawsons in Chapter 3:** They bought before they left. The close was not in the cabana. The close was in the first

three minutes of the tour, at the practice area, when Hank realized I had seen Noah correctly and Noah realized I had taken his sport seriously. By the time we walked back to sign the contract, the decision had been waiting on us for eighty minutes.

- **Brian and Rachel in Chapter 4:** Brian signed eleven minutes after the identity audit. The eleven minutes were not the decision being deliberated. They were the decision being absorbed. Brian had decided when he realized the audit was true. The silence was the close. The signature was Brian making peace with the close he had already reached.
- **Mario and Maria in Chapter 5:** Maria signed first. Mario signed after her. The close happened before either signature, in the moment Maria said, "You asked what was going through my mind. No one had ever asked me that before. Everyone just talks to Mario." That line was the close. The signatures were the formality.
- **Walter and Diane in Chapter 6:** Diane's nod. Walter's handshake. The decision happened in the silence between the food-from-the-table question and the nod. The contract was signed inside of twenty minutes. The actual close took less than five seconds and produced no audible language at all.

Seven closes. Seven different rooms. Seven different industries-of-buyer.

Not one of them was closed by a technique.

Every one of them closed at a moment the rep saw and honored. The asking, when it happened, was a single plain sentence delivered after the room had already reached its decision.

This is what closing actually is.

The Simplest Possible Ask

Three lines, in floor rotation. Each one fits a different kind of room.

- **The Plain Ask:** "If this works for you, we have a deal. Are we doing this?" Used when the room has clearly arrived but the buyer has not yet volunteered the next step. The rep names the decision plainly and invites the buyer to confirm. No ornament. No urgency. No technique.

- **The Assumptive Close—Done Correctly:** "How would you like to handle the deposit today?" This is the canon's most-named and most-misused closing technique. Used as a *technique*, it is run on schedule by rookies regardless of what the room is doing, and it scares away deals that would have closed under a plainer ask. Used as a *recognition*, when the room has clearly already decided and the conversation is now about implementation, it's one of the cleanest closes available. The veteran is not assuming. The veteran is *naming* what has already happened. (The difference between the assumptive close as technique and the assumptive close as recognition is the difference between a rookie and a veteran. The line is the same; the reading underneath it is not.)
- **The Food-From-the-Table Ask:** "If this monthly payment is within your budget, and it doesn't take food from the table, are you our new owners?" My own line, found at a closing table in my first years on the floor. Used when the math has been honestly worked through and the rep wants the buyer to feel that the deal won't be allowed to hurt their household. The ethical clause is the line's whole purpose. It tells the family that the rep would rather they walk than sign something that would erode their security. Buyers who hear this kind of clause respond to the respect underneath it, and they usually sign.

Three variants. One principle. The veteran reads the room and picks the line. The line is small. The reading is everything.

The rookie's instinct is to find the one perfect closing line and run it on every deal. There is no such line. The veteran has three or four lines and chooses contextually, the way the veteran chose between Family A and Family B questions in Chapter 4 and the way the veteran chose which story to tell in Chapter 6.

The reading is the move. The line is the formality.

What the Rookies Get Wrong

Four common failures, named cleanly.

- **Running a Closing Technique on a Schedule:** The rookie has been trained to close. The training said to close at the end. The end is at minute eighty-eight. So the rookie runs a closing technique at minute eighty-eight whether the room is ready or not. The veteran closes when the room is ready, which might be minute forty-five or minute one hundred and ten—or never, in which case the veteran walks honestly rather than forcing a deal that will be rescinded on Monday morning.
- **Mistaking Enthusiasm for Readiness:** The rookie sees the buyer engaged and warm and thinks the deal is ready to close. Warm isn't ready. Engaged isn't ready. Engaged-and-warm with a small partner-look and a leaned-back posture *is* ready. The signals are specific. The rookie reads only the easiest ones, and the false positives cost them deals.
- **Closing Too Softly:** The opposite rookie failure. The rep has been so polite, so consultative, so afraid of being seen as a pusher that they never actually ask. The conversation ends with "take some time, let me know what you decide"—and the deal dies of softness. Tracy was right about this. The rep who cannot ask is the rep who never closes. The middle is where the deals live: plain, calm, asking when the moment arrives, walking when it doesn't.
- **Trying to Recover a Missed Closing Moment with More Pitch:** The closing moment passed. The buyer hesitated. The rookie now pitches harder—more features, more urgency, more reasons to say yes. The veteran does the opposite. The veteran goes quieter—"Tell me what's not landing for you." The harder pitch closes nothing. The quieter question opens the conversation back up to the truth.

The Field Drill

In your next sales conversation, don't run a closing technique. At all.

Pay attention instead to when the closing moment arrives—or whether it does.

Watch the leaned-back posture. Watch the partner-look. Listen for the volunteered logistical question. Notice when the guarded body language relaxes. Sit in the silence after a substantive question.

When you see the moment, ask plainly. Pick the line that fits the room. "If this works for you, are we doing this?" Or "How would you like to handle the deposit today?" Or "If this monthly payment is within your budget, and it doesn't take food from the table, are you our new owners?"

If the moment doesn't arrive, don't force it. Name the absence honestly. "I don't think we're at a yes today. What would have to be different for this to be one?"

After the meeting, audit yourself.

- Did the closing moment arrive? If yes, did you read it correctly?
- If you read it, was your ask plain or ornamented?
- If the moment didn't arrive, did you walk the deal honestly or did you force a close that the room wasn't ready for?

Run the drill for one month. Count the closes you got from reading the room versus the closes you forced with technique. The math will tell you what the chapter has been arguing.

Another note for honesty before we go.

The seven closes in this chapter all happened. They closed in the rooms I've described. The walks—the deals that didn't close—are not in this chapter and are not in Part I. The closing technique that scared off a deal that should've closed, the forced ask that produced a rescission inside the cooling-off window, the conversation that ended in a polite no when a plainer ask might have produced a yes—those stories exist. I have lived them. They will be addressed in a later chapter of this book, in the context of what a career of walks does to a salesperson and what the math of those walks teaches over time.

Part I has shown you the work as it lands when the rep reads the room correctly. Part II will engage the books that claim to explain the same work.

What Part I Has Argued

We have now walked through seven chapters together.

Chapter 1 named the axis the canon has been wrong about for forty years—transactional and complex, not small and large. Chapter 2 took you through the first ten seconds. Chapter 3 took you through the warm-up. Chapter 4 named the question families that no canon book has assembled. Chapter 5 took you to the table and showed you who at that table was the actual deal. Chapter 6 named the storytelling craft that closes more rooms than any technique the canon has cataloged. And this chapter, Chapter 7, has argued that the close itself is not a technique but a recognition.

The argument across all seven chapters is one argument:

> **The craft is older than the books. The floor has been running this work for a century, generation by generation, veteran to rookie, in rooms that the books were never inside. The veterans can't always articulate what they're doing. The books arrived later, named pieces of the craft, and convinced their readers that the named pieces were the whole work. But the named pieces were never the whole work. The whole work is the seven moves the rep makes in sequence in every conversation that closes—reading the quadrant, reading the first ten seconds, running the warm-up, asking the right questions, reading the table, telling the right story, recognizing the closing moment—and the discipline that holds all seven together.**

That discipline is the craft.

The craft is what Part I has been about.

Now we leave the floor for a while.

Part II is about the books—the sales canon as it has been written from outside the work. Carnegie, Cialdini, Voss, Pink, Rackham, Dixon, Tracy. The seven authors. The handful of foundational texts every working salesperson is expected to have engaged with, and the ones a serious book about sales is expected to take seriously.

I take them seriously.

Part I has been the craft as the floor has run it for a century.

Part II is what the books say about the same work.

We'll see who has it right.

Part II—The Science begins on the next page.

Chapter 8—The Other Side of the Table—the buyer's psychology, from a vantage point no major sales book has occupied.

PART II

THE SCIENCE

CHAPTER 8
THE OTHER SIDE OF THE TABLE

"We're at a point where time matters more than money. I'd rather spend it making memories with them than sitting at home saving it."

That sentence was said to me by a man in his seventies, sitting next to his daughter at the closing table of a vacation ownership package he had just decided to help his family buy. I had been in the room with him for about ninety minutes. He had been one of the quieter ones in the group. And then he had said that single sentence, and the room had changed, and the deal had closed.

I've been thinking about that sentence ever since.

Not because of what it told me about him. Because of what it told me about how little I—after twenty-one years on sales floors—actually knew about what was going on inside the heads of the buyers I had been closing.

I knew the moves. I knew the signals. I had spent two decades reading body language, listening for hesitation, watching for the look between partners that meant the household had silently decided. I could tell you, from across a tour line, which families were going to buy and which ones were going to walk.

What I could not tell you, with the same confidence, was *why*.

This chapter is my attempt to answer that question honestly. Not from the seller's side of the table, where I have spent my entire career, but from the buyer's side, where I have never sat—and where, until

I started having the conversations behind this chapter, I had never thought to ask.

What This Chapter Is

Every sales book in print is written from the seller's view. Every framework. Every taxonomy. Every set of moves and techniques. The literature of selling is, almost without exception, the literature of *what the seller does*—and the buyer appears in it as an object the seller acts upon. A type to be classified. A profile to be matched. A resistance to be overcome.

This is not a moral complaint. Sales books are written by sellers for sellers, and the seller's vantage point is the natural one for the genre. But it produces a strange blindness. The literature can tell you, in immense detail, what to *do* to a buyer. But it can tell you almost nothing about what the buyer is *experiencing* while you're doing it.

I wanted to know.

So I asked.

Over the past several months, I went back to five buyers I had closed with—across vacation ownership, real estate, and mortgage origination—and I asked them what was actually going through their heads during our conversations. Not what they had told me at the time. Not the polite version. What they were *really* thinking—before they walked in, during the meeting, and in the days and weeks after they signed.

What they told me changed how I think about this work.

The seller's view of a sale is the view from outside the buyer's head, looking for signals about what's happening inside. The buyer's view of the same sale is something else entirely—a quiet, often unspoken conversation the buyer is having with themselves about whether to execute a decision they were, in most cases, already privately carrying.

I want to share what they said, in their own words, with their names changed to protect their privacy. Then I want to talk about what their stories, taken together, reveal about a side of this craft the canon hasn't yet looked at.

Tom, Jen, and Harold: The Ohio Family

A family of six visiting from Ohio came in during spring break of 2025. Husband, wife, two young kids—Kai was four, his older sister six—and the wife's parents. They had toured the resort because the wife's mother had heard about it from a friend and wanted to take a look. They had told themselves, very explicitly, that they were "just looking."

By the end of the afternoon, the husband, the wife, and the wife's father had jointly purchased a shared ownership package.

Months later, I asked them what had actually been going through their heads.

The husband—Tom—laughed. "Honestly, I came in ready to say no. I told my wife in the parking lot, 'We're not buying anything today.' I've sat through these before, and I thought I had it figured out."

He paused.

"But this felt different. It didn't feel like we were being pushed—it felt like we were actually planning something."

The wife—Jen—said her shift had come earlier than her husband's. "For me, it clicked when I saw the kids already acting like this was 'our place.' They weren't asking if we were leaving—they were asking when we were coming back. That kind of hit me."

Then she said something that took me a moment to absorb.

"We've talked for years about doing more trips with my parents while we still can, but we never actually plan it. Life just gets in the way."

The wife's father—Harold—had been the quietest of the three during the tour. He had asked a few questions. He had listened more than he had spoken. And then, near the end, he had said the sentence I opened this chapter with: "We're at a point where time matters more than money. I'd rather spend it making memories with them than sitting at home saving it."

When I asked him months later why he had said that when he had said it, his answer was simple. "I had been thinking it for about a year. I had just never said it out loud. Something about how the conversation was going made it feel like the right place to say it."

Tom said the line that has stayed with me longest of any in this chapter. I asked him what had really moved him from the parking-lot *no* to the closing-table *yes*. His answer:

"What got me wasn't the property—it was the idea of splitting this with them. I never even considered that. Once you said that, it stopped feeling like a big expense and started feeling like a shared commitment."

The deal closed because three people who had each been carrying a private intention—Tom's openness despite the bravado, Jen's regret about postponed family trips, Harold's year-long unspoken thought about time and money—found themselves in a room together where those intentions could finally surface and be acted on.

I hadn't changed their minds. I had given them a way to act on minds they had already changed in private, separately, for months and years before they walked in.

Greg and Lisa: The Texas Couple Who Already Knew

A couple from Texas, mid-fifties, had bought a small vacation ownership package about five years before they came back to see me in 2010. They weren't planning to upgrade. They came in, as the husband put it, "to see what's new."

They left with a larger package, a more flexible plan, and a structure that finally matched how they had actually been using the property for years.

When I asked Greg, the husband, what had been going through his head, he was direct. "We weren't planning to upgrade. Not even a little. We came in thinking this was just going to be an update meeting, maybe grab a few perks and head out."

Then he said something most reps never hear from a buyer.

"I've always been cautious with this stuff. I already said yes. I don't like being sold twice."

The wife—Lisa—had a different perspective entirely. "I already knew we had outgrown what we bought. We were running out of points halfway through the year and either cutting trips short or paying extra. It started to feel backward—like we owned it, but still had to limit how we used it."

She paused.

"That part was frustrating."

Two things in what Lisa said are worth pausing on.

First, she had *already known* they had outgrown their package. Not after I had pointed it out. Not after I had run the math. She had known before they walked into the room. She had been frustrated, in silence, for some unspecified period of months or possibly longer. The conversation we had was the conversation she had been having with herself, quietly, for a long time.

Second—and this is the part most reps miss—she had not told her husband. Or if she had, she had not made it a real conversation. The frustration was hers. The decision to do something about it had to be his too. And the meeting we had was the structure within which that quiet household conversation could finally take place out loud.

I didn't sell Greg and Lisa anything they didn't already want. I gave them a setting in which Lisa's quiet frustration could become a household decision. The upgrade was the artifact of a conversation that should have happened in their kitchen six months earlier—but hadn't.

That is what I'm learning to understand about this work. Most of what I've been doing for twenty-one years is not persuading. It's creating the room where buyers finally act on decisions they'd already made in private.

Andre: The Caribbean Investor

In mid-2006, a man in his early forties from the Caribbean came to me about acquiring an eight-unit rental building in central Florida. He was experienced in multifamily real estate in his own country. He wanted long-term cash flow and US market exposure. He needed financing support, documentation across two countries, and a price that would make the math work.

The deal took weeks. It involved multiple rounds of negotiation, lender coordination, and the slow assembly of a financial paper trail that worked across two regulatory systems.

I hadn't spoken to Andre in years when I called him for this chapter. He answered on the second ring.

"At the beginning, I assumed this wasn't going to work," he told me. "Too many moving parts. Different country, different rules, and every step felt like another document, another delay. In my experience, when it gets this complicated, deals usually fall apart."

I asked him when his thinking had shifted.

He thought about it for a moment.

"The financing part was the biggest question for me. I have the capital, but proving it the way the bank wants—it's not simple when your accounts, income, and taxes are in another country. There were moments I thought, 'This is not worth the effort.'"

He went on. "I wasn't trying to win an argument on price. I just needed the numbers to make sense. At the original price, the return didn't justify the risk for me. When we finally got close to my number, that's when I started taking it seriously. Before that, it was just a conversation."

Then he said the line that has reshaped how I think about long-cycle deals.

"What changed for me wasn't the price—it was the follow-through. You stayed in it the whole time. Most people would've lost patience or pushed me to rush. Instead, we solved each piece. That gave me confidence the deal would actually close, not just look good on paper."

I have closed many deals across many quadrants. I had assumed, for most of my career, that the close was made at the moment the buyer said yes. But Andre taught me something different. For complex multi-meeting deals, the close happens somewhere in the *middle* of the process—at the moment the buyer privately decides that the deal is going to actually happen, because the rep across from them has demonstrated the patience and discipline to see it through.

After that moment, the close is paperwork.

Before that moment, no amount of paperwork will produce a close.

I didn't know this from the seller's side. I had been operating, all those weeks with Andre, as if the close was still being made every time we got on the phone. The truth is that Andre had already silently decided, at some unspecified moment a few weeks in, that the deal was going to close *if I didn't stop showing up.* The rest was just the working out of the details.

Ryan and Emma: The Cruise Package

A young couple in their late twenties came in on a cruise-and-land package that required them to attend a tour of the property as part of the experience. They had not chosen to look at vacation ownership. They had chosen a cheap cruise package, and the tour had been the price of the cheap cruise.

They became owners that same afternoon.

When I caught up with Ryan and Emma several months later and asked what had really been going through their minds, they spoke about it in a way that surprised me.

"The biggest thing for us," Ryan said, "was that this is actually the kind of travel we want to do more of. The vacation felt fun, easy, and realistic. We could already picture ourselves building a lifestyle around trips like this."

Emma added, "We could see ourselves doing this every year. Not just once, but at least one full week every year."

The word that came up over and over in their conversation was *commitment.*

"We always talk about taking more vacations, but then life gets busy and we end up spending the money somewhere else," Emma said. "This gave us a way to actually protect that decision."

Then Ryan said the line that made me realize what had really happened in our conversation.

"We weren't really asking if we were going to spend the money. We already knew we would. The question was whether we wanted to spend it with a plan or just keep doing it randomly."

The most striking thing Ryan said came at the very end.

"We thought this was going to be a big decision, but it really just made sense."

I want to be careful with this last sentence because it's doing something profound.

Ryan had walked into the room expecting a *big decision*—the kind that requires deliberation, anxiety, second-guessing, and possibly a few sleepless nights. What he had found instead was *recognition.* The product he was looking at was the structured version of a decision he and Emma had already made about how they wanted to live. The conversation he had with me didn't produce that decision; it gave him a way to see, clearly, that the decision had already been made.

When the close came, it was not a *deciding* moment; it was a *recognizing* moment.

This is what Joe was running in 1989. This is what veterans on every commissioned floor in America have been running for a hundred years without ever quite naming. The buyer is, in most cases, not deciding. The buyer is recognizing.

The rep's job is to make the recognition possible.

Dr. Bennett and Jessica: The Physician Couple

About nine years ago, a young physician fresh out of residency, and his wife who was nearly finished with her own residency, toured a $750,000 home—four bedrooms, three baths, two-car garage, and a pool. They were renting at the time. They told me, almost immediately, that the home was probably too much for them.

The deal closed because we ran the actual math and qualified him for a VA loan.

When I caught up with Dr. Bennett—the name I'll use for him here—and his wife Jessica recently, their reflections on what had really been happening in their heads were the most honest single window into a young household's interior decision-making that I have had in this whole project.

"Our first thought was, 'This is a beautiful house, but it's probably more home than we should take on right now,'" Dr. Bennett said. "We had just spent years training, and the idea of jumping into something that expensive felt risky."

Jessica was more specific. "We loved the house immediately, but we kept telling ourselves to be practical. We were comparing it to our rent, not to what the house would actually cost us long-term."

She paused.

"Once we saw the numbers, it stopped feeling unrealistic."

There is a quiet word in what Jessica said that does most of the work in the sentence: *unrealistic.*

She had walked into the house carrying a story about what was *realistic* for her household at that moment in their careers. The story said, "We're young, we just finished training, and we shouldn't buy a house at this price." The story wasn't stupid—it was responsible. It was the kind of story careful people tell themselves to protect their financial future.

The problem with the story was that it had been built from incomplete math.

When we ran the numbers—and when Dr. Bennett qualified for a VA loan with payments that landed close to what they were already paying in rent—the story collapsed. Not because we had argued with it, but because the new math revealed that the story had been comparing the wrong things.

Jessica said it cleanly: "We were comparing it to our rent, not to what the house would actually cost us long-term."

Most buyers I have worked with were comparing the wrong things. They were comparing the purchase to their savings rather than to their lifetime cost of *not* purchasing. They were comparing the new payment to their current payment rather than to their future earning potential. They were comparing the cost of the decision to the comfort of not making it, rather than to the cost of staying in their current situation.

My job, in most cases, was to help them see what they were actually comparing—and to give them the math that let a private intention become a public decision.

Dr. Bennett and Jessica have been in that house for nine years. They have raised children there. They have refinanced once. The home is now worth significantly more than what they paid. None of that would have happened if Jessica had stayed inside the "unrealistic" story she walked in with.

She didn't stay inside it because the actual math was put on the table in front of her.

That is most of what I do.

The Pattern Across All Five

I sat down with the transcripts of all five conversations after I had collected them, and I carefully read through them, analyzing what they had shared.

What I found was a single pattern, present in every conversation, that I had never seen named in any sales book:

Every one of these buyers was carrying a deeper intention that they hadn't executed.

Look closely:

- Tom and Jen had been talking for years about doing more trips with Jen's parents while they still could. They hadn't executed. Harold had been thinking for a year about time and money but hadn't said it out loud.
- Greg and Lisa had outgrown their vacation ownership package and were managing the frustration in silence. They hadn't had the conversation.
- Andre had been trying to get into the US real estate market and dealing with the friction. He had been close to walking away.
- Ryan and Emma were already serious about annual travel as a household priority. They just didn't have a structure for it.
- Dr. Bennett and Jessica were privately considering buying a home but kept telling themselves a story about what was realistic.

None of these buyers needed to be convinced.

Every one of them needed help executing a decision they were already privately carrying.

That single sentence reshapes how I think about everything in this book.

When I read the room in Chapter 2, what I'm actually reading is *whether the buyer has a deeper intention to surface.* When I run the warm-up in Chapter 3, what I'm actually doing is *creating conditions where a private intention can become public.* When I ask the truth questions in Chapter 4, what I'm actually doing is *helping the buyer articulate what they have already been carrying.* When I read the table in Chapter 5, what I'm actually identifying is *which person in the room is closest to executing the intention the household has been delaying.* When I tell a story in Chapter 6, what I'm actually doing is *showing the buyer a version of themselves who has already executed.*

Sales is not persuasion.

Sales is helping the buyer execute the decision they were already carrying.

I want to be careful with this claim because it can sound naive. Of course some buyers come in genuinely undecided. Of course some are not yet ready and walk for honest reasons. Of course some are persuaded by something they had not considered. The pattern is not universal.

But it's closer to universal than the canon has acknowledged.

The buyer who closes is, in most cases, a buyer who walked in carrying something they had been quietly thinking about, and who found in the conversation with the rep the structure they needed to act on it. The rep who understands this is doing fundamentally different work than the rep who is trying to convince the buyer of something new.

The veteran has known this for a long time, without language.

The buyers, when asked, name it directly.

Cialdini, Seen from the Receiving Side

Robert Cialdini's *Influence*, first published in 1984, names the seven principles that have shaped persuasion theory for the last forty years. Reciprocity. Commitment and consistency. Social proof. Authority. Liking. Scarcity. And unity, added in the expanded edition.

The book is foundational. It's also, almost without exception, written from the seller's side.

I want to look at the seven principles once, briefly, from the side of the buyers I just heard from. Not to dispute Cialdini. To examine what the canon has missed by always writing from the seller's chair.

Reciprocity

- Cialdini's argument: Humans feel an obligation to give back when they have received something. Sellers can deploy this by offering small gifts, samples, or favors.
- From the buyer's side, this principle is real—but the buyers I spoke with didn't describe it as obligation. They described it

as *recognition* that the rep had treated them as a person rather than as a transaction. Andre's "You stayed in it the whole time" isn't just gratitude; it's recognition of professional discipline. The reciprocity is real. It's just not what the canon thinks it is.

Commitment and Consistency

- Cialdini's argument: Small commitments lead to larger ones because humans want to be consistent.
- From the buyer's side: Ryan and Emma's story is the cleanest example. They had been making the *unstructured* version of the commitment—taking vacations, spending the money—for years. The ownership purchase didn't start a commitment. It *recognized* one they had already been making, in fragmented form, for as long as they had been a household.

Social Proof

- Cialdini's argument: People look to others to determine appropriate behavior.
- From the buyer's side: The social proof that closed Tom, Jen, and Harold was not from other buyers. It was from each other. *They* were each other's social proof. The grandfather's willingness to say what he said gave the husband and wife permission to commit to what they had been postponing. The social proof was internal to the household.

Authority

- Cialdini's argument: People defer to credentials and expertise.
- From the buyer's side: Jessica and Dr. Bennett deferred to the math, not to me. The VA loan qualification was authority. My role was to surface it. The authority was in the financial reality, not in the seller's expertise. The veteran rep is an *interpreter* of authority, not the holder of it.

Liking

- Cialdini's argument: People are more easily persuaded by those they like.
- From the buyer's side: None of the five buyers used the word *like* to describe their decision to work with me. They used words like honest, patient, follow-through, and transparency. The canon's *liking* is the floor's *respect*—and Chapter 9 has already named what the canon got wrong by conflating them.

Scarcity

- Cialdini's argument: Limited availability increases perceived value.
- From the buyer's side: None of the buyers I interviewed cited scarcity as a factor in their decision. Not one. Either scarcity was less important than the canon claims, or the buyers themselves didn't perceive it as a factor even when it was operating. Both possibilities are worth sitting with.

Unity

- Cialdini's argument: Shared identity creates a persuasive pull.
- From the buyer's side: Harold's "shared commitment" line is a unity moment. The deal closed because three generations of one family saw themselves as a single unit acting together. Cialdini was right about unity. He undersold it. It's not one principle among seven—it is, for households, *the* principle.

Cialdini was right about most of what he named.

But what he missed, by writing from the seller's side, is the *register* in which the principles operate. From the seller's side, they look like levers to be pulled. From the buyer's side, they look like quiet internal alignments that the rep either honors or violates.

The rep who tries to *deploy* Cialdini on a buyer is operating in the wrong register. The rep who recognizes the principles already operating *inside* the buyer's interior life—and respects them—is operating in the right one.

That distinction is not in *Influence.* It comes from sitting on the other side of the table and asking.

What the Buyers Wish Reps Knew

When I asked each of these five buyers the catch-all question—"Is there anything you wish I had asked you that I didn't?"—their answers, taken together, point to something the canon will not say out loud.

They wished reps would *trust them more.*

Specifically, they wished reps would trust that they had already been thinking about the decision before they walked in. They wished reps would stop performing persuasion on them when what they actually needed was the structure within which to execute. They wished reps would understand that the buyer who looks resistant is often, internally, much closer to a yes than the rep realizes—and that what the buyer is resisting is not the deal but the *pressure*, the *performance*, the *sense of being acted upon.*

Tom said it most directly. "I came in ready to say no. What changed it was that nobody tried to change my mind. We just talked about what made sense."

Lisa said it with frustration. "I wish someone had asked me, five years ago, whether what we bought was working for how we actually traveled. Not just 'Are you happy?' but whether the product matched the usage. I would have told the truth. I had been frustrated for years."

Andre said it about long-cycle deals. "Most people in your position want to control the pace. The deal closed because you let me set the pace and showed up at every step."

Ryan said it about urgency. "We thought we were going to be pressured. We were ready for it. The reason we bought that day was that we never were. So we got to decide for the right reasons."

Jessica said it about the math. "I wish someone had told me, before we ever sat down with you, that comparing our rent to the home's mortgage was not the actual comparison. That the actual comparison was much more complex. We almost didn't take the meeting because we thought we already knew the answer. We didn't."

What runs through all five answers is a quiet plea:

Trust that we are adults who know our own lives. Help us see what we're not seeing. Don't try to convince us of something we haven't decided yet. Help us execute what we are already, privately, ready to do.

That is the chapter.

That is what no sales book has yet said clearly, because no sales book has asked yet.

What This Changes

I have been writing this book from the seller's side for chapters 1 through 7. Every move, every framework, every closing technique has been described from the vantage point of the rep across the table.

This chapter is the only one written from the other side. After this chapter, the book returns to the seller's view for the rest of its length—Chapter 9's Challenger framework, Chapter 10's Voss toolkit, the rest of Part II's canon engagement, and Part III's technology.

But the book is different now.

Every chapter that follows this one has to be read through what these five buyers said. The Challenger move from Chapter 9 isn't teaching the buyer about themselves—it's helping the buyer surface what they were already privately thinking. The Voss labeling from Chapter 10 isn't naming the buyer's emotion as a technique—it's giving the buyer language for what they had been carrying silently. The closing moment from Chapter 7 isn't the moment the rep extracts a commitment—it's the moment the buyer recognizes that the private decision has now become a public one.

The seller's craft doesn't change.

What changes is what the craft is *for.*

It's not for moving buyers across decisions they hadn't made. It's for honoring the decisions they were already, quietly, in their interior lives, ready to act on—and giving them the room within which the act could finally take place.

The veteran on the floor has been doing this all along.

The buyers, when finally asked, name it directly.

That is the chapter.

Next chapter: Challenger Beyond B2B—what Dixon and Adamson found in the corporate world, what they missed about consumer sales, and the move every working rep has to learn from the discipline they named.

CHAPTER 9
CHALLENGER BEYOND B2B

I had a real estate agent on my team named Rob.

Everyone liked Rob.

He was super friendly. Always checking in with clients. Always *building relationships*. People enjoyed talking to him.

But for the life of him, he couldn't close anything.

He brought me a deal once. Buyers had been looking at houses with him for a few weeks. He said they "just needed more time." That was his explanation every time something didn't move forward.

I asked him, "What did you actually say when they told you that?"

He kind of shrugged it off. "I told them, 'No problem, take your time. I'll send you more options.'"

That right there was the problem.

I told him straight up, "That's why you're not closing. You're helping them stay stuck."

He didn't love hearing that. He pushed back. Said he didn't want to come off pushy, didn't want to ruin the relationship.

"You're not protecting the relationship," I explained. "You're avoiding the moment when they actually have to make a decision. And because of that, they never do."

Then I gave him something to say.

I told him, "Next time they say they need more time, don't agree with it. Ask them why. And don't accept a surface answer."

A few days later, he has the same situation. The buyers say, "We just want to think about it."

This time, instead of backing off, Rob says, "What exactly are you trying to figure out? Because we've already seen enough homes for you to know what you like."

The buyers hesitate.

Then they admit they are nervous about making the wrong decision.

Now it's real.

Now it's not "We need more time." It's fear.

From there, Rob can actually walk them through it. Talk through the risk. Help them make a call.

They moved forward on the deal.

Afterward, Rob came back to me and said, "That felt completely different."

That was when it clicked for him.

Being nice was not the issue.

Avoiding tension was.

The moment he stopped trying to keep things comfortable and started digging into what was actually holding the buyer back, everything changed.

That was the shift—from being liked to actually being effective.

What Dixon and Adamson Found—and What They Missed

In 2011, Matthew Dixon and Brent Adamson published *The Challenger Sale.*

They had run the largest sales-rep study since Rackham. Over six thousand reps. Nineteen companies. The kind of empirical work that takes years to produce and that almost nobody else in the canon was doing.

What they found was uncomfortable for a generation of sales managers.

They identified five rep profiles. The Challenger. The Lone Wolf. The Hard Worker. The Reactive Problem Solver. And the Relationship Builder.

Then they ranked them by performance.

The Challenger was the top profile—40 percent of star performers. The Lone Wolf was second. The Hard Worker was third. The Reactive Problem Solver was fourth.

The Relationship Builder was dead last. Only 7 percent of star performers. The worst-performing profile of the five.

That finding broke a lot of training programs. The canon had spent forty years telling reps to *build relationships.* Dixon and Adamson had just shown that the reps who built their whole strategy around relationships were the ones who couldn't close.

I read the book when it came out. I recognized everything in it. I had been managing rooms full of those five profiles for years. The numbers in their study matched what I had been watching on consumer floors my entire career.

But Dixon and Adamson had only studied B2B. Enterprise sales. Corporate buying committees. Their book was written for that world.

The framework they built applies to consumer sales too. They just didn't say so, because they didn't study it.

That is what this chapter is about.

The Challenger is real. Dixon and Adamson named it for B2B, but the same profile exists on every commissioned consumer floor in America and runs the same way. The Relationship Builder is real. Dixon and Adamson named it for B2B too. And the consumer floor has the same problem—friendly reps who never close, who underperform their peers, who wash out by year three, and who never quite figure out why.

The framework is portable. The book just never moved it.

I am moving it now.

The Same Five Profiles, on a Consumer Floor

The five profiles look like this in the rooms I have managed.

- **The Challenger:** The rep who pushes back. Disagrees with the buyer when the buyer is wrong. Asks the hard question and lets it sit. Takes control of the conversation without being aggressive. Frank, in Chapter 6, wasn't running this profile when he came to me. But he learned to. The closer the book has called Joe, "the grand daddy," has been running this profile his entire career.

- **The Lone Wolf:** The rep who closes on pure instinct. Doesn't run the script. Can't be coached on anything. Constantly about to get fired—and constantly saving themself with one more deal. Every floor has one. They close. They are also impossible to scale and usually leave on their own terms.
- **The Hard Worker:** The reliable middle. Runs the script. Calls back. Follows up. Most reps are Hard Workers. The floor needs them. They won't break into the top 10 percent, but they make their numbers, and the company runs on their consistency.
- **The Reactive Problem Solver:** The customer-service rep. Solves what the buyer asks them to solve. Polite, helpful, responsive. Closes the buyers who already know what they want when they walk in. Underperforms with buyers who don't.
- **The Relationship Builder:** Rob. Friendly. Liked by everyone. Builds rapport that feels real. Always checking in. Always sending follow-ups. The buyer leaves the conversation feeling good about the rep. And the deal never closes.

Dixon and Adamson's number for the Relationship Builder was 7 percent of star performers. Twenty-one years on consumer floors tells me that number is about right. Maybe a little high. The Relationship Builders I have managed have almost never been top closers. The ones who survived their first two years became something else—usually Hard Workers, sometimes Challengers if they had a good mentor. The ones who stayed Relationship Builders washed out.

That is uncomfortable to read. Most consumer floors have Relationship Builders right now. Some of them are reading this. The book isn't telling them that they're bad people; it's telling them that the strategy they're running is the strategy that doesn't close.

The fix is not a personality change.

The fix is the Challenger move.

What the Challenger Actually Does

Dixon and Adamson described the Challenger by what they teach the buyer: *teaching for differentiation.* The B2B Challenger walks into the room and teaches the buying committee something they didn't know about their industry, their operations, or their market. The teaching reframes how the buyer sees their own situation. The deal closes because the buyer now sees something they didn't see before.

That move works in B2B because the rep often knows things about the buyer's industry that the buyer does not.

But it doesn't work the same way in consumer sales.

A family buying a vacation ownership package doesn't need to be taught about the vacation ownership industry. A couple buying their first home doesn't need to be taught about the housing market. A retired engineer buying a second home doesn't need to be taught about real estate trends. Most consumer buyers have already done their research before walking into the room. Trying to teach them about *the market* makes the rep look like they're running a script.

But there's a different version of the Challenger move that works in consumer sales. It has been running on commissioned floors for a century. Dixon and Adamson didn't name it because they weren't looking at consumer sales.

I will name it here:

The consumer Challenger teaches the buyer about themselves.

Not about the product. Not about the market. About the buyer's own situation. Their own fears. Their own decision. Their own life.

For Brian, in Chapter 4, the identity audit was a consumer Challenger move. "Is the fear of repeating your father bigger than the fear of losing your wife's respect?" That was teaching Brian something he didn't yet see about himself.

Walter and Diane, in Chapter 6—the Cleveland story was a consumer Challenger move. The story showed them a version of themselves four years from now that they hadn't yet seen. The teaching wasn't about the product. It was about their own postponed life.

Rob's question to his buyers—"What exactly are you trying to figure out?"—was a consumer Challenger move. It pushed past the surface objection and forced the buyers to name their actual fear. That is teaching the buyer about themselves. The buyer didn't know what was really holding them back until Rob pushed past the polite version.

Every consumer Challenger move has the same shape.

The rep sees something the buyer has not yet seen about themselves.

The rep names it.

The buyer recognizes it.

The buyer now has to deal with it.

That is the move. The B2B canon hasn't named it, but the floor has been running it for as long as there have been sales floors.

The Four Things a Challenger Does

Four characteristics every Challenger rep runs. The list is short on purpose. Most reps fail at the Challenger move not because the move is complicated but because the four things require a discipline most reps do not have.

- **Teaches the Buyer About Themselves:** Not the product. Not the market. The buyer. "Here is what's really in your way. Here is the math you haven't faced yet. Here is the decision you keep avoiding." The teaching is direct. It is also kind, when delivered correctly. The rep is on the buyer's side, and the buyer feels it.
- **Takes Control of the Conversation:** The Challenger decides what the conversation is about and when it changes phase. Not aggressively—structurally. The buyer can talk about anything they want, but the rep is in charge of the flow. Most reps surrender control without knowing it. They let the buyer set the agenda. They follow the buyer's questions instead of leading them somewhere. The Challenger leads. The buyer follows the lead and feels guided rather than steered.
- **Is Willing to Disagree:** This is the discipline most reps cannot do. The buyer says something that's not true—about the market, about their situation, about what's in their way—and the Relationship Builder agrees. "Yeah, you're right. That's a real concern." The Challenger does not. "That's not actually what would happen if you waited." / "That's not the

math your situation supports." / "That objection is not what's in your way." The disagreement is calm. It's not combative. It's honest. The buyer hears it and respects the rep for being willing to risk the comfort of the room in service of the buyer's actual decision.

- **Asks the Hard Question and Sits With It:** The fourth family from Chapter 4—the diagnostic questions and the conditional closes—all live here. The Challenger asks, "What's really keeping you from saying yes today?" The Challenger asks, "What exactly are you trying to figure out?" The Challenger asks the question and then says nothing. The Relationship Builder fills the silence with reassurance. The Challenger sits in it.

Four moves. None of them complicated. All of them uncomfortable for reps who default to friendliness as their primary strategy.

The discipline is what is hard. Not the moves.

Why Relationship Builders Fail

This is the section that is going to be uncomfortable for some readers. I'm going to be direct anyway, because the chapter cannot land at half-strength.

Buyers do not buy from reps they like.

They buy from reps they respect.

That sentence is going to upset Relationship Builders. The Relationship Builder has spent their career being told that *people buy from people they like*. The training said it. The mentors said it. The friendly culture of most sales floors reinforces it. And every Relationship Builder has personal evidence that buyers do enjoy talking to them.

But enjoying a conversation is not buying a contract.

The Relationship Builder gets warm conversations. They get high satisfaction scores from buyers who *did not buy*. The buyers liked them. But the buyers didn't respect them enough to sign.

Liking is a social emotion. Respect is a competence emotion. They're not the same, and they don't always travel together.

The Relationship Builder optimizes for liking and assumes that respect follows. It does not. Respect requires moments of constructive tension. Respect requires the rep to risk the comfort of the room for the buyer's actual benefit. Respect requires the rep to be willing to disagree, to push back, to say something the buyer didn't want to hear but needed to.

The Relationship Builder cannot do this. The reflex is too strong. *Don't risk the relationship. Don't introduce friction. Don't be the pushy one.* The reflex feels like a virtue, but it's actually a trap.

Rob had been running that trap his whole career. He thought he was being a good agent by sending more options and giving the buyers space. But he was not being a good agent; he was helping the buyers stay stuck.

The moment he asked one hard question—"What exactly are you trying to figure out?"—the buyers' actual fear came out. From that point on, Rob was being a good agent. Because being a good agent meant being willing to say something the buyers *needed* to hear, not something they *wanted* to hear.

The fix for the Relationship Builder is not to become cold. It's not to become aggressive. And it's not to give up the warmth that makes them likable.

The fix is to add the four Challenger moves on top of the warmth.

Warmth and tension can coexist. The Challenger is not unfriendly. And interestingly, the Challenger is *more* on the buyer's side than the Relationship Builder is—because the Challenger is willing to tell the buyer the truth. The Relationship Builder is willing to comfort the buyer. There's a difference, and the buyer feels it even when they can't name it.

Rob came back to me after that deal and said, "That felt completely different."

That sentence is the chapter.

The conversation felt different because the relationship was different. Rob had stopped being the agent who told the buyers what they wanted to hear. He had become the agent who told them what they needed to hear. The buyers respected him for it. They signed.

This is the move every Relationship Builder needs to learn. The warmth stays. The tension gets added. The respect follows.

How the Challenger Move Changes by Quadrant

The framework is the same in every quadrant. The content of what the Challenger teaches changes.

- **Quadrant 1—Small, Transactional:** The Challenger move is small. A retail clerk who pushes back on the buyer's first choice with a better fit—"That one's nice, but I'd actually look at this one for what you're describing"—is running a Challenger move in three seconds.
- **Quadrant 2—Large, Transactional:** Stories, identity audits, the hard question. The tour-line work. Brian's identity audit. The Cleveland story. The chapter's classic territory for consumer sales.
- **Quadrant 3—Small, Complex:** The Challenger move stretches across meetings. The rep teaches the buyer something at meeting one, lets it sit, returns at meeting two, and asks what the buyer has done with it.
- **Quadrant 4—Large, Complex:** Dixon and Adamson's home territory. Teaching the buying committee about market dynamics. Taking control of the deal cycle across months. Their original framework. Rob's deal was Quadrant 4 by structure—a multi-week real estate transaction with stakeholder consultation—and the Challenger move there looked like asking the hard question that the buyers' polite objection was hiding.

Four quadrants. Same four characteristics. Different content. The veteran reads the quadrant and runs the right version.

What the Rookies Get Wrong

Four common failures:

- **Defaulting to Relationship Builder Because It Feels Safer:** The most common failure on consumer floors. The rookie has been trained to build rapport. The rookie doesn't know that rapport without tension is incomplete. The rookie spends two years being friendly and never closes, and one of two things happens: either the rookie figures out what Rob figured out, or the rookie washes out.

- **Mistaking Aggression for the Challenger Move:** Some rookies hear "take control" and "push back" and turn into closers from a 1980s training film. Loud. Aggressive. Theatrical. That is not the Challenger move. The Challenger is calm. The pressure is internal to the conversation, not external to the buyer. The veteran's challenge is quieter than the rookie's friendliness, not louder.
- **Teaching the Product Instead of Teaching the Buyer:** The rookie who has read *The Challenger Sale* and is running it on a consumer floor often falls into this. They start teaching the buyer about the *product* or the *market*, and the buyer pulls back because the buyer didn't come to be lectured. The B2B move does not port. The consumer move is to teach the buyer about *themselves*. That is what closes.
- **Avoiding Constructive Tension Because It Feels Rude:** The Relationship Builder reflex. *Disagreement is uncomfortable, so I won't disagree.* The veteran knows that disagreement is sometimes the most respectful thing a rep can offer. The rep who never disagrees is not protecting the relationship. They are avoiding the moment that would have built one.

The Field Drill

For one week, audit yourself by the five profiles.

After each sales conversation, write down which profile you ran. Be honest.

If you closed, you were probably a Challenger or Lone Wolf. Sometimes a Hard Worker. Almost never a Relationship Builder.

If the deal stalled, you were probably a Relationship Builder. Friendly. Helpful. But not enough tension.

If your week shows mostly Relationship Builder conversations and few closes, the chapter has just diagnosed something.

Again, the fix is not a personality change.

The fix is the small move toward constructive tension in your next ten conversations.

One disagreement. One hard question. One moment where you say "I don't think that's actually the issue here" instead of "I understand."

Track what changes in your conversion rate over the next thirty days.

The math will tell you what the chapter has been arguing.

Rob ran a Challenger move that afternoon for the first time in his career.

He still had the warmth that made everyone like him.

He just stopped trying to *protect* it at the moment when the buyer actually needed something more from him.

The hard question. The pushback. The willingness to say what the buyer didn't want to hear.

That was the shift—from being liked to being effective.

The two are not the same. They're not even close.

The reps who learn the difference become closers.

The reps who don't learn it never quite figure out why their numbers won't move.

Next chapter: The Toolkit Was Already on the Floor—reading Chris Voss from the practitioner's vantage point, and naming the moves veterans were running before the FBI gave them language.

CHAPTER 10
THE TOOLKIT WAS ALREADY ON THE FLOOR

In Chapter 4, there is a moment I want you to look at again.

Brian is sitting across from me. He has just stalled the deal with the line about the math having to work: $8,000 a month on the rental—anything more is a no. I've done the math on the napkin. The number comes in lower than what they are already spending. I have slid the napkin to him.

He is reading it.

I am about to ask him the conditional close. The deal could close right there, on the math alone. But something in the room tells me the math is not the real issue.

Before I ask the conditional close, I say a single sentence.

"You probably research every major decision for weeks before buying anything, don't you?"

Brian looks surprised. Then he laughs. "Pretty much."

I nod and say, "Yeah. I figured if I pushed too hard today, you'd probably distrust the whole thing."

The room changes.

That sentence—"You probably research every major decision for weeks"—is a Voss move.

Specifically, it is *labeling*. Tactical empathy. I named what Brian was experiencing before he had to name it himself. I told him I saw him—that I understood he was the kind of person who needed time and information and that I wasn't going to push.

I didn't learn that move from Chris Voss. I had been running it for fifteen years before *Never Split the Difference* was even published. So had Joe. So had Rick. So had every veteran closer on every commissioned floor in America.

This chapter is about that.

What Voss Named in 2016

Chris Voss spent his career as a hostage negotiator for the FBI. By the time he retired and started writing, he had spent decades inside rooms where the wrong sentence could end someone's life. The toolkit he developed in those rooms was—among other things—the most concentrated body of attention-paying technique ever assembled in one job description.

In 2016, he wrote *Never Split the Difference.*

The book did three things at once. It codified a set of conversation moves that hadn't been cleanly codified before. It gave them memorable names—labeling, mirroring, the accusation audit, calibrated questions, "that's right" versus "you're right," the late-night FM DJ voice. And it grounded the moves in the gravity of life-or-death negotiation, which made readers take them seriously in a way they might not have if the examples had come from a sales floor.

All three of those things were valuable. The book deserved every bit of the reception it got. Voss is now, ten years after publication, the single most quoted modern voice in sales and negotiation training in America. He earned that position.

But the moves were not invented in 2016.

The moves were already on the floor.

What Voss did was give the canon language for a craft tradition that was older than the language.

This is the most generous chapter of Part II, because Voss got more right and missed less than any other author the book engages. His mistakes are not in *what* he said. They are in what readers sometimes conclude from how he said it—that the toolkit is for adversarial high-stakes situations, when in fact it's for the much more common terrain of ordinary collaborative human conversation.

The chapter you are reading right now is going to do two things. It is going to credit Voss properly for the naming. And it is going to walk you through the toolkit one move at a time, showing you where each move has already appeared in this book—sometimes in scenes I wrote without ever using Voss's vocabulary, because the moves themselves are older than the words.

By the end of the chapter, you'll have the Voss vocabulary in hand. You can go back and reread any chapter in this book and watch the toolkit running.

That is what Voss's gift actually was. Not the invention—the naming.

The Toolkit, Reread

There are five Voss tools that matter most for sales work. The rest of his book is excellent, but these five are the ones a working rep should be able to deploy on Monday.

I'm going to name each one. Then I'm going to show you where it has already appeared in this book.

Labeling

A label is a sentence that names what the other person is feeling or thinking, in their place, before they have to name it themselves.

The opening: "It sounds like . . ." / "It seems like . . ." / "It looks like . . ." Then the rep names the buyer's emotion, situation, or concern directly:

- "It sounds like you've been burned by a salesperson before."
- "It seems like the timing isn't working for your family right now."
- "It looks like the price isn't the actual issue."

The label does two things. It tells the buyer that they've been seen. And it externalizes the emotion or concern, which often reduces its grip on the buyer. A feeling named is a feeling that loses some of its power. The buyer who has just had their fear labeled doesn't have to carry the fear silently anymore. The fear is now in the room. The rep can address it.

Where you've already watched labeling in this book:

The Brian moment at the top of this chapter—"You probably research every major decision for weeks before buying anything, don't you?" That is a label dressed as a question. I named what Brian was experiencing and let him confirm or deny it. He confirmed it. The deal opened up.

Maria's question about the rate lock in Chapter 5, after which I said, "That's a great question," and then immediately added, "We're closing on day thirty. You'd have to delay twice to hit the lock expiration. That almost never happens. But if it did, *we* would eat the extension fee, not you." That paragraph contains an implicit label—*I see that you're worried about being on the hook for an extension fee, and I'm going to address that worry directly.* I didn't say the label out loud. The structure of my answer *was* the label.

In the Author's Note, when Joe asked the family their children's names and then used the children's names twice as often as the husband's name, that was labeling without language. Joe was saying *I see who actually runs the energy of this family.* He never had to put it in words. The labeling was in the choice of whose name to repeat.

Labeling can be spoken or structural. The veteran does both.

Mirroring

A mirror is repeating back the last few words the other person said.

- "We need to think about it."—"You need to think about it?"
- "It's a big decision."—"A big decision?"

The mirror does what a label does—confirms that the rep heard the buyer—but it does it more quietly. The mirror invites the buyer to keep talking. To explain. To unpack what they meant. Most buyers will fill the silence after a mirror with information they hadn't planned to give. The mirror doesn't pressure. It opens.

Where you have already watched mirroring in this book:

Chapter 2 has an entire section called "Mirroring Before Mirroring." The argument was that veteran reps run the mirror as an unconscious match—pace, tone, posture, energy—long before they ever learn the technical move of repeating the last few words. Rick was mirroring the husband's careful watchfulness throughout the cabana scene before he ever ran the labeling question. The technical mirror is downstream of the deeper one.

In Chapter 5, the moment Maria said "He'll want to see the origination fees line by line" and I said "Good. I'll highlight them. Anything else he'd flag?"—the phrase "anything else he'd flag" is a soft mirror. I used her vocabulary back to her (*flag*) to signal that I had heard her language and was operating within it. She offered the next concern without prompting (*prepaids, escrow*) because the soft mirror had invited her to keep talking.

In Chapter 6, when Diane said "Thank you for not making us feel stupid," I didn't mirror that explicitly out loud—the chapter notes that I didn't know what to do with the line at the time—but I did mirror it internally. The reader watches a mirror happen in the author's interior even though the conversation has ended.

Calibrated Questions

A calibrated question is an open-ended question that puts the burden of solving the problem on the buyer rather than on the rep. The classic Voss formulations begin with *how* or *what.*

- "What would have to be true for this to work for you?"
- "How would your spouse react if I told her that?"

The calibrated question is a soft pushback. It doesn't say no. It doesn't say yes. It simply asks the buyer to figure out the answer themselves, which means the buyer ends up doing the rep's work on the rep's behalf.

Where you have already watched calibrated questions in this book:

Chapter 4's entire framework on Family A and Family B questions is Voss territory by another name. The diagnostic questions—"What's keeping you from saying yes today?" / "Other than money, what else would stop you from moving forward?"—are calibrated questions. The conditional closes—"If we could structure your ownership comfortably within your budget, would we move forward today?"—are calibrated questions of the *what would have to be true* variety, structured for commitment-extraction rather than diagnostic discovery.

The identity audit with Brian—"Is the fear of repeating your father bigger than the fear of losing your wife's respect for saying no to something she clearly wants?"—is the most aggressive calibrated question in the book. It puts the entire weight of resolution on Brian. The rep doesn't solve anything. Brian solves it. The question makes him.

Rob's question to his real estate buyers in Chapter 9—"What exactly are you trying to figure out? Because we've already seen enough homes for you to know what you like"—is a calibrated question. Rob's pre-coaching version ("No problem, take your time. I'll send you more options.") avoided the calibrated question entirely. The chapter's whole argument was that the calibrated question is what Rob needed to learn.

The Accusation Audit

The accusation audit is the move where the rep preempts the buyer's objection before the buyer raises it. The rep names the worst version of what the buyer is probably thinking and puts it on the table first.

- "You're probably worried I'm going to spend the next hour trying to upsell you on something you don't need."
- "You're probably thinking this sounds like every other sales call you've gotten this month."
- "You're probably wondering whether I'm going to disappear after the contract is signed."

The accusation audit defuses the objection by naming it. The buyer can no longer hold the objection silently—it has been named out loud, by the rep, in a tone that invites the buyer to acknowledge it. Once acknowledged, the objection is in the open and can be addressed honestly. Held silently, it sits in the room as a wall the rep cannot see.

This is one of the most useful moves in the entire Voss toolkit and one of the most underused on consumer sales floors. Most reps never run it because naming the worst version of what the buyer might be thinking feels risky. The veteran knows that the opposite is true. The unnamed objection is the dangerous one. The named one is workable.

Where you have already watched the accusation audit in this book:

The opening line I gave to Brian after he disclosed his father's story: "Okay. That's not a math problem. That's a marriage problem. And I can't solve that for you." The phrase "I can't solve that for you" is an accusation audit. It names what Brian was probably afraid I would try to do—solve his identity-level problem with a sales pitch—and tells him I will not. He relaxed because the worst version of what I might do had just been taken off the table.

When I told Frank in Chapter 6: "Never prejudge. You gain nothing." Frank was probably braced for me to humiliate him in front of the family or to tell him he was bad at his job. The fact that I led with the lesson instead of with a takedown was an accusation audit. The worst thing he was probably expecting did not happen, which made him able to hear the actual lesson.

In Chapter 5, when I told Maria, "That's actually smart. Most people don't," about her father reviewing the numbers—that was preempting her likely fear that I would dismiss her father as a deal-killer. Naming the worst version (*I will treat your father as an obstacle*) and refusing it (*I think his review is the smart move*) was an accusation audit running underneath the larger absent-stakeholder move.

"That's Right" vs. "You're Right"

This is Voss's most quoted single distinction.

"You're right" is what the buyer says to make the rep stop talking. It is dismissal dressed as agreement. The rep hears "you're right" and thinks the deal is close. But the buyer who said "you're right" is mentally already past the conversation.

"That's right" is something else entirely. "That's right" is the buyer recognizing that the rep has accurately named something the buyer was experiencing. It is the moment of *recognition*—the same moment the storytelling chapter named as the close.

The veteran knows the difference. "You're right" means walk the deal. "That's right" means the deal is alive.

Where you have already watched "that's right" in this book:

Walter and Diane's silence after the Cleveland story was a "that's right" moment that didn't need to be said out loud. They recognized themselves in the story. The recognition was visible. Diane was looking at her hands. Walter was looking at me. Neither one said the words "that's right," but the room had reached the moment.

Brian's eleven-minute silence after the identity audit was a "that's right" moment. He wasn't deliberating whether the audit was true. He was absorbing that it was true. The silence was the recognition.

Maria's nod, after the divorce-fear revelation, was a "that's right" moment. She wasn't agreeing with a proposition. She was confirming that the conversation had finally reached the truth.

The buyer doesn't always say the words "that's right." The veteran reads the recognition in the body, in the silence, in the look between partners. The words are not the move. The recognition is.

Where the Hostage Frame Helps, and Where It Limits

Voss came up as a hostage negotiator. The cases that anchor his book are some of the most consequential negotiations in American law enforcement history. Bank robberies. Kidnappings. Cases where the wrong sentence ended someone's life.

That frame gave the toolkit gravity. A reader who watches a tactical empathy move work in a kidnapping scenario understands that the moves are serious. They are not soft skills. They are real tools that operate at the level of life-or-death decision-making.

That gravity helps the book land. Sales books have a credibility problem, and Voss's life-or-death cases bypass the credibility problem entirely. By the time the reader has watched a hostage negotiation succeed, they take the toolkit seriously enough to deploy it in lower-stakes situations.

But the frame also limits the toolkit in a small way that matters.

Some readers come away thinking the toolkit is only for adversarial situations. For confrontation. For high-stakes moments where the rep is dealing with a difficult counterparty. They reserve labeling and the accusation audit for moments they perceive as conflictual.

That is wrong.

The Voss toolkit is the everyday craft of paying attention to another human across a table. It is for collaborative rooms, friendly conversations, warm tours, family meetings about a real estate purchase, and mortgage closings with people who have already decided to work with you. The hostage frame in the book is the *most extreme example* of where the toolkit works. The toolkit's primary application is everywhere else—the ordinary rooms where a rep is trying to help a family make a real decision.

The Cleveland story was a Voss-style move running in a room full of warmth, with no adversary anywhere in sight. Walter and Diane were not the rep's opponents; they were the rep's family for ninety minutes. The toolkit landed in a friendly room because the toolkit's job is to deepen attention, not to overpower resistance.

The reader who applies Voss only to adversarial situations is using one percent of the toolkit's value. The veteran applies it everywhere.

What the Rookies Get Wrong

Three common failures:

- **Running Labels Mechanically:** The rookie reads Voss, learns the "it sounds like . . ." opener, and starts running it as a verbal tic. Every sentence the buyer says gets a label slapped on it. "It sounds like you're saying the price is high. It sounds like timing is an issue. It sounds like your husband isn't ready yet." The buyer reads the rep as having learned a technique and is now performing it on them. The labels lose their power because they're no longer connected to actual attention. The veteran labels rarely, and only when a real emotion or concern is in the room. The label lands because it's earned.
- **Running Mirrors Without Attention:** Same failure on a different tool. The rookie repeats the last few words back as a technique, disconnected from real listening. The buyer feels the artifice. "We need to think about it."—"You need to think about it?"—"Yes, that's what I said." The mirror doesn't work

because the rep is mirroring as a maneuver rather than as a deepening of attention. The veteran's mirror always carries real curiosity. The buyer feels the difference.

- **Targeting "That's Right" as a Goal:** Voss talks about "that's right" as a milestone the rep should be working toward. Some rookies read that and start trying to *produce* a "that's right" moment by manipulating the conversation toward it, but the buyer feels the manipulation. The veteran doesn't target "that's right." The veteran is paying attention to whether recognition is happening in the room—and "that's right," when it comes, is read as a signal rather than aimed at as a target. The difference is subtle. The buyer feels it anyway.

The Field Drill

Pick one Voss tool.

The strongest candidate for most reps is labeling. It is the move with the highest return on the lowest learning curve.

For the next ten sales conversations, deploy one label per conversation. Just one. Use the "It sounds like . . ." or "It seems like . . ." opener and name something real that you're noticing about the buyer.

- "It sounds like the math is not your actual concern."
- "It seems like your spouse has more questions than you do."
- "It looks like you've been through a presentation like this before."

Then stop talking.

Listen to what the buyer says next. Most buyers will fill the silence with information they hadn't planned to share. Some buyers will deny the label and offer the truth instead. Either response advances the deal more than the conversation you would have had without the label.

After ten conversations, audit yourself.

- Did the labels land?
- Did the buyer's posture shift after you named something?
- Did the conversation deepen?

The math of these conversations will tell you what Voss has been arguing—and what the floor has been arguing for longer than Voss has.

Voss didn't invent the toolkit.

He named it.

The naming was the gift. The toolkit was already on the floor.

Joe was running labels in 1989. Rick was running mirrors in the parking lot before families opened their car doors. Every veteran closer on every floor has been running calibrated questions since long before Voss gave them the vocabulary.

What changes when you read Voss is that you now have words for what the veterans have been doing in front of you. You can deploy the moves on purpose. You can train the moves into newer reps. You can recognize the moves when other reps run them on you.

That is what canon books are for. They give the floor language for what the floor has been doing.

The mistake is reading Voss—or any of the seven authors of the canon—as the inventor of the moves.

The veterans were running these moves before the books were written.

The books named what was already on the floor.

Next chapter: The 80/20 Is Real (And Mostly Mental)—what Brian Tracy got right about self-concept, what the canon misses about wash-out, and why the top 20 percent of every commissioned sales floor takes home most of the money.

CHAPTER 11
THE 80/20 PRINCIPLE IS REAL—AND MOSTLY MENTAL

I remember the exact moment the file changed.

I was at the table with Robert and Denise. Both buyers. Real estate deal. The contract was in front of us. We had been through everything. The numbers were on paper.

Robert looked up and said, "The price is too high."

Old me would've started softening the edges. Trying to save the deal by giving ground too early. The Relationship Builder reflex from Chapter 9—the instinct to keep the room comfortable by walking the price back.

This time, I didn't.

Instead, I mirrored.

"You think the price is too high," I said.

I didn't phrase it as a question. I said it as a statement. I gave him back what he had said and then waited.

He nodded. Said they had other options.

"Then let's talk about those options," I replied. "Because if they gave you this same value, this same upside, and this same path to close, we wouldn't still be here."

I didn't concede the price. I didn't negotiate. I named the test that Robert's own behavior was already failing: *If a better option existed, you would already be there.* Robert was still at my table, which meant the alternatives were not actually equal. The objection was real, but it was not the real obstacle.

That was the shift.

I stopped negotiating to avoid losing the deal and started leading the room like the broker I was.

Denise went quiet. Robert looked back at the contract.

Then he said, "All right. Let's do it."

The deal closed.

And that conversation became part of the file I carry now.

I don't back off from hard objections.

I repeat them. I address them head-on. I close through them.

This chapter is about why that conversation mattered.

It's also about why the chapter you are reading is the chapter most reps need most. Not because of what I said to Robert, but because of what I had stopped doing inside my own head before I sat down at his table.

It wasn't about believing I could close the deal that afternoon.

It was about *seeing that it already closed.*

That distinction is the chapter.

The Inner Game Is the Game

There was a time when I thought sales was mainly about words, timing, and technique.

I believed that if I said the right thing at the right moment, the deal would naturally happen.

That belief held for a while. It held through my early years on the tour line. Through the first promotions. Through the first stretch where I thought I had it figured out.

Then I started losing deals I should've won. And winning deals I had no business winning.

The pattern took years to see clearly.

On the days I felt uncertain, that energy showed up. The buyer felt it. The room felt it. The script didn't matter—I could deliver it word-for-word and still leave with nothing. On the days I felt clear, grounded, and certain, people responded differently. Same script. Same product. Same hour of the day. Different results.

That's when I understood that we do not just speak our thoughts—we live them. The buyer reads the version of you that walked in the door long before they hear the version of you reading the pitch.

That changed everything.

I started paying attention to the thoughts I was repeating. Because those thoughts were shaping my confidence, my presence, and my influence. The buyer doesn't buy a product. The buyer buys certainty. The buyer buys trust. The buyer buys the feeling that the person across the table believes in what they are offering.

Once I understood that, I stopped trying to force sales and started leading with stronger thinking. I trained my mind to expect opportunity. To stay calm under pressure. To show up with conviction whether the last tour had walked on me or closed for the year's biggest deal.

The mind changed first. Then the results.

The veterans on every floor I have ever worked knew this. Most of them couldn't articulate it; they just walked in with it. The reps who washed out in the first twelve months—and most of them did—washed out because nobody told them that the inner game *was* the game.

Tracy was right about self-concept. Pink was right about buoyancy. The floor was right too.

Every sale begins with the story you tell yourself first.

The 80/20 Principle Is Real

The math of every commissioned sales floor I have ever worked on follows the same shape.

Typically, 20 percent of the reps produce roughly 80 percent of the revenue. Some floors are more compressed: top 10 percent producing 70 percent. Some are slightly looser: top 30 percent producing 75 percent.

The exact ratio varies, but the phenomenon is universal.

This is not unique to vacation ownership. It happens in mortgage origination. In real estate. In auto sales. In insurance. In pharmaceutical sales. In financial advisory work. In every commissioned environment I have ever observed or worked alongside.

The bottom half of any new-hire class is gone within eighteen months. Not because they're lazy. Not because they're stupid. In fact, many of them are smart. But they washed out because the math of the floor caught them—they could not produce at the rate the floor required.

The middle stays stable: the Hard Workers and the Reactive Problem Solvers from Chapter 9. They make their numbers. They don't break into the top 20 percent. They don't wash out. They are the floor's backbone—and most reps on most floors are in this category.

Then there is the top 20 percent.

These are the closers. The reps who hit the numbers year after year. The names everyone on the floor knows. The reps the manager assigns the toughest tours to, because the manager has watched them survive tougher tours and come out with contracts.

The variable that separates them from the rest is what the chapter you are reading is about.

It's not talent. Top closers come in every shape—quiet and loud, fast and slow, polished and rough. Some of the best closers I have ever managed couldn't write a coherent email. Some of the worst could deliver a flawless pitch.

It's not training. Most floors run the same training program for everyone. The wash-outs got the same training the closers got.

It's not territory. The same prospect cards get assigned to top closers and to wash-outs across the same year. The difference in conversion is not in the leads.

It's not luck. Across enough conversations, the luck averages out. The top 20 percent don't get lucky for twenty consecutive years.

And it's not even hours. The top closer doesn't work twice as many hours as the wash-out. Sometimes they work fewer.

The variable is internal.

Brian Tracy named this in 1988. He called it self-concept.

He was right.

He was also, in my view, slightly incomplete.

What Tracy Got Right, and What the Floor Sharpens

Tracy's argument in *The Psychology of Selling* was that the rep's self-concept governs their performance ceiling. The rep cannot earn more than they have decided they are worth. The rep cannot close at a higher rate than their self-concept supports. The rep cannot break into the top 20 percent without first becoming the kind of person whose self-concept allows the top-twenty-percent income.

This is true. Twenty-one years on commissioned floors have confirmed it repeatedly to me. I have watched reps stay stuck at a specific income level for years, even when their skill was visibly improving. I have watched other reps double their income in eighteen months without any obvious change in technique. The variable in both cases was what they had decided was true about themselves.

Tracy named the variable correctly.

What he left abstract is what self-concept actually is—and that abstraction is where the motivational genre Tracy founded has lost most of its working value.

The genre's standard answer is *belief*: Believe in yourself. Have a positive attitude. Visualize success. Affirm your worth.

The advice isn't wrong, exactly. It is just too vague to be useful to a rep on a Monday morning who has to walk into a tour at ten o'clock.

The floor's version is sharper: Self-concept is not what you *believe* about yourself. It's what you've decided is true.

The two are different.

Belief is fragile and contingent. It depends on the day. The mood. The last deal. The week's numbers. The argument you had with your spouse last night. Belief is what you do when you don't yet know.

Decided truth is harder. It doesn't move easily. It comes from somewhere belief doesn't come from. It comes from accumulated evidence—from the file the veteran has built over hundreds of conversations—that they have already done the thing they are about to do again.

A veteran doesn't *believe* they can close the deal in front of them.

A veteran *sees the deal already closed.*

The closing happens, in their head, before the conversation has reached the closing moment. They walk into the room having already lived the outcome. The conversation is the catching up of the external world to the internal already-completed event.

You can only believe if you do not know.

The closer knows.

The rookie believes—when the rookie is doing well—but belief is unstable. A bad week destroys belief. Belief doesn't survive sustained pressure.

What survives pressure is the file. The accumulated evidence of what you have done under pressure before. The veteran is not running on belief. The veteran is running on a thousand previous conversations where they held their nerve and the deal closed because they did. The file is the operating system. Belief is the user interface.

This is what the motivational genre has missed. It's been trying to fix the user interface. But the interface isn't the problem—the operating system is.

You don't "believe yourself" into the top 20 percent.

You build the evidence file.

Then the self-concept catches up.

How the File Gets Built

Every conversation a rep has is a deposit or a withdrawal.

A deposit is a moment when the rep held the harder line. Asked the question they would normally back off from. Sat in the silence they would normally fill. Closed through the objection they would normally negotiate. Whatever the outcome—close or walk—the discipline produced a deposit.

A withdrawal is the opposite. A moment when the rep flinched. Softened the question. Walked back the price too early. Filled the silence with reassurance that the buyer hadn't asked for. Even if the deal closed anyway, the withdrawal happened. The file got slightly weaker.

The math of the file is not what most reps think it is.

Most reps assume the file is built from *wins*. Close a deal, file gets stronger. Walk a deal, file gets weaker. This is wrong. The file is built from *moments of nerve*, not from outcomes. The rep who closed a deal by flinching has weakened their file even though the deal closed. The rep who walked a deal by holding the harder line has strengthened their file even though the deal walked.

I want to be specific about this—because the canon has not been.

The Robert and Denise story above was a deposit. The deposit happened in the moment I said "You think the price is too high" without softening, and then in the moment I named the test that his behavior was already failing. Whether the deal closed or walked after that, the deposit was already in the file. The closing was confirmation. The file was already changed.

If Robert had said "You're right, we're going to look at the other options" and walked out the door, the deposit would still have been in the file. I would have left the table with a strengthened internal operating system even though I had lost the deal externally. The next conversation I walked into would have carried the file with it.

This is the math the floor runs on and which the canon mostly doesn't name.

The reps who build the file deliberately are the reps who move into the top 20 percent. They don't wait for the floor to assign them deposit-producing conversations. They make every conversation a deposit by choosing which moves to run in it. The hard question. The held silence. The unwalked-back price. The refusal to soften.

The reps who don't build the file deliberately end up with whatever file the floor accidentally produces for them. Often that file is a mix of soft deposits and harder withdrawals—enough to keep them in the middle, but not enough to move them into the top.

The reps who run nothing but the soft moves—the Relationship Builders from Chapter 9—build the wrong file entirely. Their file is full of moments where they backed off, filled silences, softened questions, and walked away from harder conversations. That file produces the rep they become. They cannot will their way out of the file through positive thinking. The file is the rep. Until the file changes, the rep doesn't change.

The Wash-Out Curve

The bottom half of any new-hire class on any commissioned floor is gone within eighteen months.

I have watched this for twenty-one years. It doesn't change. The names change, but the patterns do not.

Some of the reps who washed out were people I liked. Some of them were people I had personally trained. Some of them were people who worked harder than the closers around them. The math caught them anyway.

What washed them out was not effort. It was the file they were building.

A rep who spends a year softening hard questions, walking back prices early, filling silences with reassurance, and avoiding the conversations that would have made them uncomfortable—that rep has built a year of withdrawals. The file at month twelve is weaker than the file at month one. The rep's self-concept is now lower than it was when they started. The next twelve months are harder than the first, not easier.

This isn't a failure of character. It's structural. The floor produces this result reliably for reps who don't build the file deliberately, and the people on the receiving end of it are not always able to see what's happening.

The honest part of this chapter—the part the motivational genre won't say—is that you cannot save every rep who is on this curve. Some of them will not change the moves they're running, and so the file won't change, and they'll wash out. The manager's job is to identify the reps who can change and to coach them while there's time. The reps who cannot—or will not—change will leave the floor on their own schedule, and the floor moves on without them.

For the rep who is on this curve and reading this chapter: The path back is not motivation. The path back is one harder conversation per week. One hard question you normally wouldn't ask. One refusal to back off. One held silence. Every conversation is a deposit or a withdrawal. The deposits compound, the file builds, and the self-concept changes.

But the change doesn't start with belief.

It starts with the next deposit.

Why This Is Not Motivation

A serious reader, by this point in the chapter, may be wondering whether what I'm calling "the evidence file" is just motivation dressed up.

The distinction matters, and I want to be honest about it.

Motivation is what you *feel*. It comes and goes. It's mood. It's unreliable. The motivated rep can be unmotivated tomorrow. The motivated rep walking into a Monday morning tour after a rough weekend is sometimes not motivated at all by the time the buyer arrives at the door.

The evidence file, on the other hand, is not what you feel—it's what you've decided based on accumulated evidence. It doesn't come and go. It's what you walk into the room with whether you feel motivated that day or not.

The top 20 percent are not more motivated than the wash-outs. Sometimes they are less so. The closer who has been doing this for fifteen years often has lower motivation on any given day than the new hire who's excited about their first month on the floor. The closer outperforms the new hire anyway.

The file beats the feeling. Every day.

A rep with a strong file in a bad mood will outperform a rep with a weak file in a great mood. I have watched this happen on every floor I have managed. The motivational seminar can produce a temporary spike in the weak-file rep's numbers, but the spike doesn't hold. Two weeks after the seminar, the file reasserts itself and the rep is back where they were.

What does hold is the work of building the file. Deposit by deposit. Conversation by conversation. The harder question this week. The refusal to soften next week. The held silence the week after.

Ninety days of deliberate file-building produces a different rep.

A year of it produces a different career.

This is what Tracy was reaching for and what the motivational genre that followed him obscured. The genre tried to fix the feeling, but the feeling was never the problem. The file was the problem. The file is what you build with the next conversation, and the one after that, and the one after that.

The rep who runs this for ninety days has the proof. The rep who keeps reading more books and going to more seminars without changing the next conversation does not.

How This Changes by Quadrant

The file gets built differently in different quadrants. The principle is the same. The pacing changes.

- **Quadrant 1—Small, Transactional:** The file builds fast. A retail clerk runs hundreds of micro-conversations per week. The file consolidates in months. The wash-out curve here is the steepest—reps who can't build the file quickly can't survive this quadrant's pace at all.
- **Quadrant 2—Large, Transactional:** The chapter's classic territory. Tour-line reps build the file across a hundred to two hundred tours per year. Two to three years of deliberate file-building consolidates a working closer.
- **Quadrant 3—Small, Complex:** The file builds more slowly. Fewer deals, longer cycles, but each entry is bigger. The wash-out curve is gentler. The path to top performance is also longer—usually four to seven years.
- **Quadrant 4—Large, Complex:** Mortgage origination. Complex B2B. Real estate at the higher end. Enterprise sales. The file builds over years. Top performers in Quadrant 4 often have decades-long careers before the file is fully consolidated. The math of this quadrant rewards patience.

The principle is the same in every quadrant. Every conversation is a deposit or a withdrawal. The file is built, not believed. The reps who break into the top 20 percent build it deliberately.

What the Rookies Get Wrong

Four common failures:

- **Mistaking Belief for Self-Concept:** The rookie reads Tracy and tries to will themselves into the top 20 percent through positive thinking. The belief doesn't survive a single bad week. The file would have held. The rookie has not built the file.

- **Avoiding the Conversations That Build the File:** The hardest conversations are where the deposits happen. The rookie who avoids the hard conversations—who keeps running the soft moves, who keeps backing off the close, who keeps softening the question—is choosing to build a different file than the one that produces closers. The choice is invisible at the time. The result shows up a year later in the income.
- **Treating Wash-Out as Personal Failure:** A rep who washes out at month fourteen did not fail morally. They failed to build the file fast enough to survive the math of the floor. This is structural, not personal. Reps who wash out and understand this can move into other work without the corrosive self-blame that the motivational genre tends to produce. Reps who don't understand it carry the wash-out as a personal verdict for years afterward. The book is doing them a service by naming the truth.
- **Believing That Talent Alone Explains the Gap:** The most common mistake among middle-tier reps. *The top closer was born that way. I was not. The gap is fixed.* This is wrong. The gap is built. The middle-tier rep who decides to start building deliberately can move into the top 20 percent in three to five years. They almost never do, because the file-building work is uncomfortable and the talent-belief is comfortable.

The Field Drill

Pick the next conversation on your calendar where you know—already, before it starts—that there will be a moment when you would normally back off.

Maybe it's the buyer with the absent stakeholder. Maybe it's the partner who hasn't spoken. Maybe it's the moment you would normally soften the close. Maybe it's the price objection that you would normally negotiate away too early.

Decide right now that you will not back off this time.

Run the harder question. Sit in the silence. Hold the price. Repeat the objection back to the buyer and address it head-on the way I did with Robert.

Whatever happens—whether the deal closes or walks—write it down at the end of the day.

One sentence:

- "I held the harder line. The deal closed."
- "I held the harder line. The deal walked, but I learned what was really in the way."

Do this every week for ninety days. At the end of the ninety days, you will have thirteen entries.

The file is now real. The rep is now different.

Then keep going.

Robert and Denise signed because I had stopped negotiating to avoid losing the deal and started leading the room like the broker I was.

That sentence describes one conversation.

It also describes a career.

Again, the veteran doesn't *believe* the deal will close.

The veteran sees that it *already* closed.

You can only believe if you do not know.

The closer knows.

Next chapter: What Quota Does to a Salesperson—the chapter the canon will not write, and the human cost of a career on commission.

CHAPTER 12
WHAT QUOTA DOES TO A SALESPERSON

Every morning for twenty-one years, I showed up to work holding a blank check.

Not a real one. Nobody handed me a piece of paper. But that's what it was. I walked onto the floor every single day with a paycheck that had no number on it. At the end of the day, I wrote the number myself. I wrote it with whatever I had closed.

If I closed, the number was real.

If I didn't close, the number was zero.

No sale, no money.

That is the truth of commissioned selling that no other chapter in this book has said plainly, and which almost no sales book ever says at all. Every other chapter has been about how to win. This chapter is about what winning costs—and what it costs the people who can't win often enough.

Because the blank check doesn't care how good your intentions are. It doesn't care how hard you worked. It doesn't care that you have a mortgage, or a kid starting college, or a parent in a nursing home. It doesn't care that you gave a great tour, built real rapport, told the right story, and the family walked anyway for reasons that had nothing to do with you.

The check is blank every morning.

You write the number every night.

You do this every day, for years, for as long as you stay in the business.

That is the job. Everything else in this book is in service of that one fact.

What the Blank Check Does to a Person

Most people have never lived this way and can't imagine it.

Most people get a salary. The number is the same whether Tuesday was a good day or a bad one. The number arrives whether they closed anything or not. The number is there when they are sick, when they are grieving, when they are distracted, when they are coasting. The salary is a floor under their feet. They stand on it without even thinking about it.

The commissioned salesperson has no floor.

Every morning, the salesperson wakes up and the number resets to zero. Whatever he did yesterday is gone. The deal he closed last week already paid out or already didn't. Today is blank. The mortgage is due on the first of the month whether today is blank or not. The family needs to eat tonight whether today is blank or not.

This does something to a person over time.

It runs a calculation in the back of the mind that never fully shuts off. Walking into a tour, the calculation is running. Driving home, the calculation is running. Lying in bed on a Sunday night before a Monday that is blank again, the calculation is running. *How many deals this month? How many tours left? What's my ratio? What happens if the next three walk? What happens if I have a bad month? What happens if I have a bad quarter?*

The calculation doesn't stop because you want it to stop. It doesn't stop on weekends. And it doesn't stop when you take time off. There is no such thing as paid time off when the check resets to zero the day you get back, which means the commissioned salesperson never fully rests, not even on the rare vacation they let themself take. It doesn't stop at your kid's recital or your anniversary dinner. The blank check follows you everywhere, because the blank check is not on your desk—it's in your head.

And the pressure finds the body.

Reps often carry it in their stomachs. In their sleep (or the lack of it). In their blood pressure. Some of the best closers I ever knew paid for the career in their health, years later, when the bill for two decades of that daily pressure finally came due. The body keeps the score even when the salesperson pretends they're fine. *Especially* when they pretend they're fine.

Nobody tells you this when you take the job.

They tell you about the upside. The uncapped income. The freedom. The cars the top closers drive. They don't tell you that the upside and the pressure are the same thing wearing two faces. The reason the income is uncapped is that there is no floor. The reason there is no floor is the blank check. You can't have the one without the other: The freedom and the weight are the same object.

The Efficiency Ratio

The blank check is the psychological reality. The efficiency ratio is the institutional one.

Every commissioned floor runs on math. Deals per month. Tours taken versus deals closed. A closing percentage the company expects you to maintain. The numbers vary by company and by product, but the structure is always the same: You have to close a certain number, at a certain rate, or you do not stay.

This isn't cruelty. It's arithmetic. The floor costs money to run. The leads cost money to generate. The space, the marketing, the support staff, the manager's time—all of it is spent on every rep, whether the rep closes or not. A rep who takes the tours and doesn't close the deals is a cost with no return. The company carries that cost for a while. Then the company stops carrying it.

The rep who couldn't hit the monthly number was gone in a short period. The rep whose closing ratio fell below the line was gone. Not because anyone hated them but because the math didn't work, and the math doesn't negotiate.

I watched this happen for twenty-one years. The pattern never changed. A new class of reps would start—eager, trained, believing this was going to be the career that changed their lives. Within a few months, the floor's math began sorting them. The ones who could write a real number on the check often enough stayed. The ones who could not started slipping below the ratio. And once a rep slipped below the ratio, the slide was usually in one direction.

The company gave them a window—a month, sometimes two—to get the number back up. Most of them couldn't. The pressure that was already crushing them got worse when the manager started having the conversations about the ratio. The worse the pressure got, the worse they closed. The worse they closed, the lower the ratio went. The lower the ratio went, the closer the end came.

Then one day, their badge didn't work and their desk was cleared and there was a new name on the board where their name had once been.

The floor moved on by lunch.

The Floor Has a Small Mercy Now

It used to be worse.

For most of the history of this business, commissioned selling meant *pure* commission. Straight commission. No base, no draw, no floor of any kind. You ate what you killed, and you starved when you didn't. The blank check was not a metaphor in those years. It was the entire pay structure. A rep could work a full month, take every tour assigned to them, do everything right, hit a cold streak, and take home almost nothing. That was legal, it was common, and it broke people fast.

That has changed over recent years.

Under the Fair Labor Standards Act, there is no minimum number of hours an employee must work to be paid a salary or to earn commission—but the law does require that most nonexempt commissioned employees be paid at least minimum wage for the hours they work. If the commissions in a given period don't get the rep to minimum wage, the employer generally has to make up the difference. The result is that more and more companies have moved away from pure commission and toward a structure of base hourly pay or a small salary, *plus* commission on top.

This matters for the rookie more than for anyone.

The salary-plus-commission structure puts a thin floor under the new rep's feet. It means that the first few months—the months when the rep is still learning the craft, still building the file, still figuring out whether this career is for them—do not have to end in a household crisis the first time the rep hits a cold streak. The rookie can pay rent while they learn. The base wage buys them time.

And time is the one thing the old pure-commission structure never gave anyone.

This is why commissioned sales is more attractive to the rookie today than it was twenty years ago, and why rookies last a little longer now before the floor sorts them. The base doesn't change the math in the end—the efficiency ratio still rules, the deals-per-month metric still has to climb, and the rep who can't eventually close enough will still be gone. But the base extends the runway. It gives the rookie enough months to find out honestly whether they can learn the craft before the math makes the decision for them.

That is a real improvement. It's more humane than what came before, and it lets people discover what they're made of without betting the rent on the answer in week one.

But make no mistake about what the base wage is. It's a runway, not a destination. Nobody builds a life on minimum wage plus a few small commissions. The base keeps the lights on while you learn, but the *commission* is where the living is made. The rep who settles into the comfort of the base and stops fighting for the close has not been saved by the new structure. They have only delayed the same conversation about the ratio that the old structure would have had with them sooner.

The floor is a little kinder at the start now.

It's exactly as honest at the end.

More Left Than Stayed

Here is the number nobody puts in the brochure.

For every rep who lasted at least five years, I watched ten come and go.

Ten.

The wash-out is not the exception in this business. The wash-out is the rule. The survivor is the exception. Most people who walk onto a commissioned floor believing they have found their career are gone within eighteen months, and the large majority of everyone who ever tries this work doesn't make it to the five-year mark.

This is the part of the job that breaks your heart if you let it, especially if you're the manager. Because some of the ten were people you liked. Some were people you trained personally. Some worked harder than the survivors did. Some had families counting on them, and you watched the blank check grind them down week after week, and you knew before they did that the math was not going to work for them, and there was nothing you could do about it except be honest with them while there was still time.

The ones who left didn't fail as people. Most of them were good people. They failed to do a specific, brutal thing often enough: walk into a room cold, with a blank check, and write a real number on it before the day was over. Day after day. For years.

That's harder than it sounds. It's harder than almost anything else people do for a living. The people who have only ever drawn a salary don't know how hard it is, because they have never stood on a floor with no floor under them.

The ten who left carried something out the door with them. Some of them carried shame they didn't deserve. Some carried debt. Some carried a marriage that didn't survive the bad quarter. Some carried a belief that they were failures, when the truth was that they had attempted one of the hardest things a person can do for money and it just hadn't worked out—which is a different thing from being a failure, though it rarely feels that way to the person carrying it.

I think about some of them still.

Why the Survivors Survived

The survivors were not lucky.

Across five years, across ten years, across twenty-one, the luck averages out. Nobody survives two decades of the blank check on luck.

The survivors survived because they had the craft.

Everything in this book up to this chapter—the reading of the parking lot, the warm-up, the questions, the reading of the table, the story that closes, the recognition of the closing moment, the file that becomes the closer—all of it is, in the end, the answer to one question:

How do you write a real number on a blank check—often enough, for long enough—to feed your family for a career?

The craft is not just how you win. The craft is how you *survive.*

The rep who masters the craft closes often enough that the check is rarely zero. The rep who doesn't master the craft closes rarely, the check is often zero, the ratio slips, and the floor sorts them out. The difference between the survivor and the ten who left is not character and not effort and not luck. It's whether they learned to do the thing this book has been teaching—and learned it fast enough to survive the math while they were learning.

That is why I wrote this book.

Not to romanticize the career. The career doesn't need romance. It needs the truth, and the truth is that it is one of the hardest ways to make a living that exists, and most people who try it don't make it.

But the ones who *do* make it—the ones who learn the craft, who build the file, who can walk into a cold room with a blank check and lead it to a close—they make a living that most salaried people will never touch.

I want to be specific about this, because the cost side of this chapter has been specific and the reward side deserves the same honesty.

The survivors I came up with own their homes outright. They put their kids through college without loans. They drove the cars they wanted, took the trips they wanted, and answered to no one about how they spent a Tuesday afternoon. They built retirement on their own terms, with money they earned with their own mouths and their own nerve, on days that started with a blank check and ended with a number they wrote themselves.

There is no ceiling on this work. That's the other face of having no floor. The same structure that washes out the ten is the structure that lets the survivor outearn the vice president who manages him, the attorney who closed his house, the doctor who treats his family. I have watched closers without a college degree make more in a year than people with two advanced degrees and a corner office—because on a commissioned floor, the only credential that pays is whether you can write a real number on the check, and that credential is earned in the room, not in a classroom.

It's one of the last careers in America where what you earn is exactly what you are worth on any given day. No politics. No waiting your turn. No ceiling someone else decided for you. You are paid for what you produce, in full, and the producing is a skill that no algorithm has yet been able to replace.

That is the deal. The blank check in the morning. The real number at night. The freedom and the weight, the same object, for as long as you can carry it.

For the ones who learn the craft, it's one of the best deals in working life.

The craft is what makes that possible.

The craft is the difference between the survivor and the ten.

The Honest Accounting

I am not going to pretend the survivors paid no price.

We did.

The survivors paid in the same currency the ten paid in. We just had enough coming in to cover the bill and keep going. The pressure was the same pressure. The blank check was the same blank check. The body kept the same score. The Sunday nights were the same Sunday nights. The difference was that we closed often enough that the math worked, and so we stayed, and we kept paying the price for another year, and another, and another.

Twenty-one years is a long time to carry a blank check every morning.

It costs something. It costs something even when you win. The survivors I know learned to carry the weight of this work without letting it break them. But learning to carry it is not the same as not carrying it. We carried it. And we are still carrying some of it. The career leaves marks on the people who succeed at it, not only on the people who fail at it.

The ones who got out whole were the ones who figured out early that the blank check was a tool, not a verdict. The number you write on it at the end of the day is a measure of *that day's work*, not a measure of your worth as a person. The reps who could keep those two things separate survived with their souls intact. The reps who let the blank check become a daily referendum on whether they were worth anything—those reps got hurt whether they closed or not. Some of the best closers I knew were also some of the most damaged, because they had tied their entire sense of self to a number that reset to zero every morning.

The craft keeps you fed.

Keeping the check separate from your soul keeps you whole.

You need both to last a career.

What This Means for You

If you're reading this and thinking about a commissioned sales career, know that I'm not trying to talk you out of it. I'm trying to tell you the truth about it, which is more than most people will.

Sales are here to stay. As long as there are products that require a human being to move another human being across a decision, there will be commissioned salespeople, and there will be blank checks, and there will be the math that sorts the survivors from the ten.

The career can be one of the best livings a person without a fancy degree or a family fortune can make. I am proof of that. So are the other survivors I came up with. We built real lives on this work. And we're not sorry we did it.

But go in with your eyes open.

The check is blank every morning. You write the number every night. No sale, no money. Most people who try this cannot carry that, and there's no shame in being one of them. But there is a great deal of pain in finding out the hard way, after you've already bet your family's security on a career that the math was never going to let you keep.

Learn the craft. Build the file. Keep the check separate from your soul.

If you can do those three things, you can survive this. You can do better than survive it; you can build the kind of life most people only get to read about—owing nothing, answering to no one, paid in full for exactly what you're worth.

If you can't, the floor will tell you, and it will not take long, and it will not be gentle.

Both of those things are true at the same time. That is the deal. That is what this career asks and what it pays. Anyone who tells you only the first half is selling you the dream. Anyone who tells you only the second half is selling you the fear. This book has tried to tell you both, because both are the truth, and you deserve the whole truth before you bet your years on it.

That is what quota does to a salesperson.

It's the most honest thing in the business.

Part II ends here. Part III—The Technology—begins on the next page, with the stack that's rewriting the job in real time and what every salesperson has to understand about it now.

PART III

THE TECHNOLOGY

CHAPTER 13
THE CRM WAS NEVER THE POINT

I have used a number of customer relationship management programs (CRMs) across two industries over twenty years.

Some have been excellent. The mortgage industry has built CRM software that does serious, professional work—tracking applications through every stage of underwriting, automating compliance reminders, organizing lender relationships, surfacing client data the moment you need it. The real estate industry has its own set of tools, equally capable in their own domain—listing pipelines, transaction management, marketing automation, lead tracking across years of slow-burn referral relationships.

This chapter is not a criticism of any CRM. I rely on these systems and wouldn't want to work without them.

Rather, this chapter is about something different. It's about a mistake that reps and managers across every commissioned industry have been making for as long as CRMs have existed—and that AI is about to make worse before it makes it clearer.

The mistake is treating the CRM as the point.

The CRM is not the point.

The CRM was never the point.

The conversation is the point.

The CRM is the apparatus *around* the conversation. The notes that remind you what was discussed last time. The calendar that tells you when the buyer asked you to follow up. The flag that surfaces the client who has gone quiet and might need a check-in. The history that lets you walk into the next meeting knowing exactly where you left off.

All of this is valuable. None of it closes a deal.

The deal is closed at the table—by the rep, in the conversation, with the buyer.

The CRM exists to support that moment. It does not produce it.

This is the chapter that opens Part III of this book, and the principle the chapter establishes is the principle that every chapter of Part III is going to be a variation on:

The tools serve the craft. They have never served anything else, and they never will.

If you remember nothing else from this part of the book—through the AI chapters that follow, through the pipeline chapters, through the chapter on what the working stack actually looks like—remember that.

The tools serve the craft.

What the CRM Is Actually For

A CRM, at its core, does five things well:

1. It stores information about people you have spoken with.
2. It schedules future actions you have promised those people.
3. It tracks the status of deals across stages of a pipeline.
4. It surfaces patterns across the data—which leads are converting, which have gone cold, which need attention.
5. And it reduces the cognitive load on the rep by externalizing the kind of remembering that used to live in a paper notebook or in the rep's head.

That fifth function is the most important and the most underrated.

A working rep who is closing real volume cannot remember everything. They can't remember which buyer mentioned a daughter's wedding next spring. Which one is waiting on an inheritance settlement. Which one had concerns about the maintenance fees that need to be addressed at the next call. Which one was supposed to receive a follow-up email last Thursday. The volume of small details a serious rep is carrying across a hundred or two hundred active relationships is more than any unaided human brain can hold.

The CRM holds it.

That is what the CRM is *for.* The CRM is the rep's working memory, externalized into a system that doesn't forget, doesn't lose notes, and doesn't show up on a Monday morning unsure what was supposed to happen this week.

When the CRM is being used well, it's invisible to the buyer. The buyer just experiences a rep who remembers the daughter's wedding, who follows up exactly when they said they would, who walks into the second meeting picking up the third meeting's worth of context. The buyer thinks the rep is brilliant. The rep *is* brilliant because they're using a tool that lets the brilliance show up consistently across every relationship they are running.

This is the CRM as it should be used.

Unfortunately, most reps don't use it this way.

Most reps use it as either a data-entry burden (filling fields because the manager will check, with no real connection to the buyer's actual life) or as a substitute for the conversation itself (treating the CRM as if the deal lives inside it).

Neither of these uses gets the value the CRM can deliver. And neither of them is the CRM's fault.

The fault is in the rep treating the CRM as the point rather than as the apparatus.

The Mistake

There is a specific way commissioned reps go wrong with the CRM, and it shows up in the same shape across every industry.

The rep treats the work as *getting the buyer into the system* rather than as *getting into the buyer's actual life.*

You can see this happen on any floor in any industry. The rep gets a new lead. The first thing they do is open the CRM and start filling in fields. Name. Phone. Email. Source. Stage. Notes. The rep is doing administrative work *about* the buyer instead of doing relational work *with* the buyer.

The administrative work is necessary. It's just not *the* work.

The work is the conversation.

The CRM exists so that the conversation can happen with the maximum possible context. The CRM exists so that when the buyer calls in three weeks, the rep doesn't start from zero. The CRM exists so that the next meeting picks up where the last one left off, with no embarrassing "remind me what we discussed" and no need for the buyer to recap their own life to a rep who should already know it.

But if the rep is spending more time *managing the CRM* than *having the conversation*, the CRM is no longer serving the work; the CRM has become the work. The buyer has become a record in a system instead of a person across a table.

I have seen this go badly in every industry I have worked in. Reps who spent forty minutes after every call updating the system instead of fifteen. Reps who treated CRM metrics as the goal—number of contacts logged, number of activities completed—instead of the conversation those metrics were supposed to support. Reps who could tell you which stage of the pipeline a deal was in but couldn't tell you what was actually keeping it from closing because they hadn't had a real conversation with the buyer in three weeks.

The CRM was doing its job. But the rep had stopped doing theirs.

This is the mistake the chapter is naming. It's not a criticism of the CRM—the CRM was performing exactly as designed. The rep had just let the apparatus become the work.

What Good CRM Usage Looks Like

The veteran rep treats the CRM the same way a surgeon treats their instruments.

The instruments are essential. The surgeon wouldn't operate without them. They are kept sharp, organized, ready to hand. The surgeon knows where every instrument is and what each one does.

But the surgeon's job is not the instruments. The surgeon's job is the operation. The instruments serve the operation. The surgeon who became obsessed with instrument maintenance—who optimized their tool layout but stopped paying attention to the patient on the table—would be a worse surgeon, not a better one.

Working reps with strong CRM discipline operate the same way.

The CRM gets updated quickly and accurately, with the minimum entries needed to support the next conversation. Notes are written for the rep's future self, not for the manager's audit. The most important fields are filled—the buyer's real concerns, the next promised action, the personal details that matter—and the optional fields are skipped if they don't serve the work.

The veteran spends ten or fifteen minutes per active relationship per week on CRM hygiene. Not more. The remaining time goes into the conversations.

The rookie often inverts this ratio. The rookie spends most of their administrative day inside the CRM and very little of their day inside actual conversations. The CRM looks impressive. But the numbers don't move, and the rep can't understand why.

The reason is structural. The CRM is not closing the deals—the conversation is. The rep who has been hiding in the CRM has been avoiding the conversation, often without realizing they are doing so.

This is one of the underrated dynamics of modern commissioned selling. The CRM, used incorrectly, becomes a place reps hide from the discomfort of actual selling. Updating fields is easy. Logging activities is easy. Picking up the phone and asking the buyer the question they've been avoiding is hard. The rep who has stalled at a particular stage of the pipeline very often discovers, on honest examination, that they have been doing administrative work to avoid doing the conversation work.

The CRM does not cause this. The CRM enables it.

The veteran's discipline is to use the CRM enough to support the conversation, and not a minute more.

What This Has to Do With AI

The CRM is the right opening for Part III because the CRM is the template for everything AI is about to do.

For the next several years—and likely the next several decades—AI is going to migrate further and further into the apparatus around the conversation. Lead generation. Outreach. Initial qualification. Scheduling. Calendar management. Follow-up cadences. Database hygiene. Pattern recognition. The mechanical work that has historically consumed a large portion of every rep's day is being absorbed into systems that do it faster, more consistently, and at a fraction of the cost.

This is real. It is accelerating. The reps and managers and companies that pretend otherwise are going to be left behind.

But the AI migration is not replacing the salesperson.

The AI migration is *redistributing the work the salesperson does.*

The mechanical front end is moving to AI. The conversation is staying with the human.

This is exactly the same dynamic the CRM established, scaled up by orders of magnitude. The CRM took the rep's notes and externalized them. AI is taking the rep's entire administrative day and externalizing it. The CRM didn't replace the rep, and AI isn't going to replace the rep either.

But there's a difference between the CRM era and the AI era that working reps have to understand right now.

In the CRM era, the rep who didn't use a CRM could still survive—they just worked harder than the reps who did. In the AI era, the rep who doesn't use AI is not going to survive. The efficiency gap is going to be too large for the unassisted rep to compete with.

This is the structural truth that the rest of Part III is going to spend several chapters unpacking. The rep who learns to work with AI as a serious instrument will outearn the rep who does not, by a margin that will widen every year. The rep who treats AI as a threat, or who ignores it, or who uses it shallowly, will fall further and further behind.

But the gap that matters most is not between reps who use AI and reps who do not. That gap will close on its own as AI tools become standard issue across every industry.

The gap that matters most—the gap that will produce the next generation of top closers—is between reps who use AI to *escape the conversation* and reps who use AI to *focus more fully on the conversation.*

The first kind of rep is the modern version of the rep who hides in the CRM. They will use AI to avoid the difficult, attention-intensive, emotionally demanding human work that this book has spent twelve chapters describing. They will run AI-generated follow-up sequences instead of having human-centered follow-up conversations. They will let AI handle outreach in registers they can't read or refine. They will outsource the buyer relationship to a system that doesn't know the buyer.

These reps will produce volume metrics that look impressive in the short term but revenue that will not catch up. They will be replaced, eventually, by the AI itself—because if a rep is doing what AI can do, AI will do it cheaper.

The second kind of rep—the rep this chapter and this part of the book is for—will use AI to take the administrative burden *off* their shoulders so they can pour the freed time and attention into the conversation—the deep human work this book has been teaching. Reading the room. Asking the hard question. Telling the right story. Recognizing the closing moment. Helping the buyer execute the decision they were already carrying.

That work is not going anywhere.

That work is, if anything, becoming *more* valuable, not less, as the mechanical work gets cheaper.

What This Means for You

If you are a working rep reading this, the principle to take from this chapter is simple.

Use the CRM. Use it well. Update it quickly, accurately, and in service of the next conversation. Spend the minimum time the system requires and the maximum time the buyer requires.

Do not let any tool—the CRM today, AI tomorrow—become a place where you hide from the work.

The work is the conversation.

The conversation is what closes deals.

The conversation is what you are paid for.

Everything else—every field, every report, every dashboard, every prompt, every automation—is the apparatus around the conversation. The apparatus is real. The apparatus is necessary. The apparatus is going to get more powerful and more efficient every year for the rest of your career.

But the apparatus is not the point.

The conversation is the point.

The conversation has always been the point.

When the CRM was new, that was true. When AI arrived, that was true. When agentic AI starts handling outreach autonomously, it will still be true. The technology will keep changing. The deeper truth underneath will not.

The veteran knows this in their body. The rookie has to learn it. The reps who don't learn it, regardless of how much technology they adopt, won't last.

The CRM was never the point.

The conversation is the point.

The conversation always was.

Next chapter: The Second Brain—using AI as the assistant every top closer always wished they had, without letting it take the work the closer should still be doing.

CHAPTER 14
THE SECOND BRAIN

It is 6:49 a.m. My coffee has gone lukewarm. I don't care, because in the last five minutes, I have done what used to take thirty.

My laptop is open to what I have come to call my AI cockpit—not a fancy dashboard, just a clean side panel where my assistant lives. I call her Iris. Iris is not a product. Iris is what I call the AI relationship I have built over the past few years across the tools I use in my mortgage and real estate practice. The name helps me think about AI the way I think about a working partnership rather than a piece of software. I will use her name throughout this chapter for the same reason.

In thirty seconds, Iris synthesized the last twelve emails between me and a young couple who have now walked away from three different properties. In another thirty seconds, she flagged a pattern I had missed—every time they ask about long-term resale value, they stop responding for exactly forty-eight hours.

Iris didn't solve the problem. She just handed me the thread. They're not afraid of the mortgage; they're afraid they'll outgrow the house in two years and get stuck.

A few years ago, that insight would have cost me an hour of re-reading, cross-referencing, and a vague gut feeling I couldn't prove. Or worse, I would have walked into the 9 a.m. showing thinking the problem was price. Now I walk in with a different question: *Tell me what "stuck" looks like to you.*

That is the gift.

Not automation. Clarity.

Before I started using AI seriously—and I have been doing so since 2023, when the tools became good enough to actually trust—my mornings were a shallow panic. Ten tabs open. Three unread lender updates. A client voicemail I would have to relisten to twice because I was already late. I was busy. But busy is not smart. Busy is chasing your own tail with a smartphone in your hand.

Now the prep work is almost silent. Three months of back-and-forth with another client, and Iris summarized it in eight bullet points before I finished my first sip. A seller's agent whose listing notes started showing the same descriptive word across multiple properties—Iris cross-referenced their last six deals and showed me that the word kept appearing on listings where the HOA later turned out to have unresolved issues. I would never have caught that. The pattern was real. The agent wasn't lying. They were using the same kind of softening language any of us might use, and the language happened to correlate with a structural problem the listings didn't disclose.

I want to be careful here. I'm not naming the specific word, the specific agent, or the specific listings. The pattern is real. The point is that AI surfaces this kind of pattern routinely now. Whatever the specific tag is in your market, in your industry, in your kind of deal, AI can find it for you. Patterns that the unaided brain cannot hold across a hundred conversations are now visible in seconds.

This is what AI gives the working rep when it is used correctly:

Time to be human again.

Not more deals. Better questions.

The ability to walk into a kitchen at 9:15 a.m. without the fog of calendar chaos and actually listen.

But here's what I've learned in the years since I started using this thing. And this is where the chapter turns.

For every pattern Iris finds, there is a trap I have almost walked into. For every hour saved, I have seen other reps lose weeks chasing AI-generated *insights* that were statistically plausible and completely wrong. I have seen relationships crater not because the AI failed but because someone trusted it with the wrong thing.

The rest of this chapter is about what it costs when you use this tool incorrectly. And the bill is never paid in dollars.

The Five Damages

Let me tell you how AI can hurt you if you're not careful.

1. It Gives You False Confidence

I have seen a version of this story play out more than once.

A good rep, ten years in the business, feeds AI a buyer's text history. AI tells him: *Client probably waives inspection. Bring up urgency.*

So he does.

Client waives inspection. Foundation turns out to be cracked. Deal blows up. The rep's reputation takes a hit too.

Why? Because AI saw a few texts where the buyer said "we love it," and one where she said she "just wanted this over with." It didn't know she was tired. It didn't know she was stressed. It just saw words.

The rep didn't call. He just trusted the pattern.

That is the first damage. AI gives you confidence that the room doesn't support—because AI can't feel the room. The pattern says "waive inspection." The phone call would have told you "take a breath before you sign anything." The rep who runs AI insights without the phone call is operating on half the information and doesn't know it.

2. It Damages Relationships

Have you ever had AI write something so clean that you almost sent it without even thinking?

I have.

A buyer asks, "Do you think this neighborhood is safe?"

AI gives a perfect answer. Crime stats. Block-level data. School zone overlays.

Sounds smart. Sounds professional.

Still wrong.

That client disappeared on me. Later I found out her son had been followed home from the bus stop the year before. She didn't want a report. She wanted me to say, "I live three blocks away. Here's my cell number. We can go look together tonight."

AI knows averages. It does not know fear.

The buyer who asks an emotional question and gets back a statistical answer feels the mismatch immediately. They may not be able to name what is off, but they feel it. They pull back. And the rep—who thought they had given a thorough, well-researched answer—never finds out why the conversation cooled.

3. It Makes You Lazy

This one is on me.

A few months ago, I let Iris summarize a seller's objections. She said: *Price sensitivity. Seller will likely counter at 3 percent below ask.*

Sounds good. Sounds actionable.

I walked into the conversation without reviewing the original notes. Missed the part where the seller had mentioned "my wife's garden" six times. *That* was what she cared about. Not the 3 percent. The backyard. The roses. The twenty years she had spent tending it. And the fact that the buyer wanted to pave over part of it for parking.

That's the kind of detail AI will sometimes flag and sometimes miss. The rep who has stopped reading the underlying material is the rep who will not catch what AI missed.

I have watched listings go to the agent who actually asked about the flowers.

The summary is not the conversation. The summary is a *compression* of the conversation. Working from the summary without the underlying material is working with a thinner version of reality than the buyer is actually living in. The rep who stops reading the source material loses the texture that closes deals.

4. It Generates Fake Apologies

You see this all the time now.

A deal falls apart. The rep fires off an AI-generated apology email. Sounds polished. Sounds respectful. All the right phrases. Acknowledges the disappointment. Offers next steps. Closes warmly.

The client reads it and knows immediately.

Why? Because it sounds too neat. Too perfect. No real voice. No real weight behind it.

You cannot outsource ownership. People try. But every time they do, trust gets chipped away—not just with that buyer but with everyone the buyer talks to about you afterward.

The hardest moments in this work are the ones where a real apology is required: the deal that fell apart because the rep missed something, the follow-up that didn't happen, the mistake the rep made. Those moments are where reputation is actually built—by reps who own what they did and write the message themselves, in their own voice, with the weight of accountability behind it.

AI cannot do this. AI doesn't have a reputation on the line. And AI is not the one who failed the buyer.

The rep who lets AI write the apology is telling the buyer, in the only language that matters, "I do not want to face you about this myself."

5. It Makes You Stop Noticing Things

This is the killer.

This is the one that undoes everything else.

Your brain starts getting soft. Why remember the kids' school names if AI can pull the district report? Why listen for hesitation if AI can flag sentiment? Why hold the texture of a conversation if AI can summarize it for you afterward?

Before you know it, you're not really working the deal anymore. You're standing there while the machine tells you what to think.

I caught myself last month. A client said, "We'll think about it." AI tagged the conversation as neutral. Maybe slightly positive.

But I heard her voice crack on the word *think*.

So I pushed. Gently. Turns out her husband had just lost overtime. They couldn't swing the monthly anymore.

AI missed it. I almost did too.

That is the damage that frightens me most. Not the dramatic blow-ups. Not the lost listings. The slow erosion of the attention that took twenty-one years to build. The rep who stops noticing things is not the rep who fails on a single deal. The rep who stops noticing things is the rep who *gradually, quietly, without noticing it themselves*, loses the very capacity that made them a closer in the first place.

You cannot un-soften a brain that has gone soft.

You can only refuse to let it soften in the first place.

The Real Talk

AI is good at things that have already been said.

It is garbage at what people are holding back.

It will save you time, sure. But it will also cost you deals if you get too comfortable and stop paying attention.

It will show you patterns. But sometimes the thing that matters is not a pattern yet.

It will make you faster. And if you're not careful, it will make you sloppy.

So this is the rule now:

Use AI to prep, but never to replace your presence.

Let it read the emails. Let it organize the noise. But once you're on the phone, in the car, at the table, face-to-face—put it down.

Look people in the eye. Ask the questions the machine cannot ask.

Because AI doesn't close deals.

People do.

Next chapter: The Pipeline Lives in the Algorithm—what AI is doing upstream of the rep, what it means for lead generation and qualification, and why the rep who understands the algorithm understands the business.

CHAPTER 15

THE PIPELINE LIVES IN THE ALGORITHM

Tuesday morning, 10:30.

A lead landed in my CRM that I had never spoken to and had never heard of. By the time her name reached my screen, the system already knew more about her than I would learn in the next forty minutes of working the deal.

The system knew her credit score, her self-reported income, the rough payment she was hoping to land at, and the three homes she had viewed on a competing real estate platform in the past hour. The system knew she had clicked into two other lender websites in the past twenty-four hours and abandoned a prequalification application on one of them earlier that morning. The system knew her debt-to-income ratio, calculated from a soft credit pull I hadn't run.

The system had scored her at 87 out of 100. *Hot.*

And the system was running a clock. I had ninety seconds to respond, or I dropped to second place on her screen. After five minutes, I lost the lead entirely to one of the three other loan officers the platform had ranked me against.

I called her in eleven seconds.

She picked up.

"Hey Dana, it's Dave with"—I named my lender. "You just looked at a loan program on my site. I saw you're eyeing homes in your area. We have first-time buyer programs with real incentives, but we need to check your debt-to-income first because it's tight. You got thirty seconds?"

She laughed. "You're faster than the other two."

"I'll send you a one-question link to pull your actual debts. Don't guess. I'll have an answer in four minutes. If it works, I'll share the incentives. If it doesn't, I'll tell you the exact number you need to pay down. Either way, you get an answer before your lunch break."

She sent the debts.

Her actual debt-to-income was 47 percent. The system had estimated 44. It was close—and it was wrong. The soft pull had missed a car lease she was carrying.

I walked her through paying down $2400 on a credit card. We closed thirty-three days later on a townhouse in the right zip code at the right number.

She still texts me photos of her dog on the balcony.

The algorithm delivered her, but the algorithm didn't close her. The algorithm didn't catch the missed car lease. And the algorithm didn't know how to host her—how to slow her down, give her one task, and promise her an answer she could trust by lunch.

That is what the rest of this chapter is about.

The Pipeline Has Already Migrated

I want to be honest about something most reps in 2026 are still pretending is not happening.

The lead you used to hunt for is now delivered to you by an algorithm.

Across every major commissioned industry I have worked in or watched, the top of the funnel has migrated to algorithmic systems. In mortgage, lender marketplaces match borrowers to loan officers based on credit profile, geography, and conversion likelihood. In real estate, aggregator platforms score buyer intent and route to agents weighted by closing history. In vacation ownership, tour generation runs through digital marketing funnels that qualify before the tour is ever booked. In B2B sales, intent data and predictive scoring systems run the entire prospecting layer. In insurance and financial advisory, it's the same pattern.

The migration is not partial. In some industries, it's mostly complete. In others, it's midstream. In none of them is it reversing.

The rep who's still working their day on the assumption that they own their top-of-funnel is operating with an outdated model of their own business. The hustle that used to find leads is now the hustle that responds to them—in the right window, in the right register, with the right preparation. The skill has not disappeared. The skill has moved.

Every working commissioned rep in 2026 needs to understand one thing about the new world:

You did not generate that lead—the system did. And the system decides whether you keep getting more of them.

What the Algorithm Decides That You Used to Decide

The decisions that used to live with the rep—or with the manager—now live with the system.

- **Which Buyer is Worth Your Time:** The algorithm has run thousands of past conversions and learned which lead profiles convert at which rates. The scored lead that lands on your screen has already been ranked. The leads the system thinks will convert get human routing. The leads the system thinks won't convert will get an automated email sequence and a six-week nurture cadence.
- **How Quickly the Buyer Gets a Human:** The ninety-second window I had with Dana is not unusual. Five-minute response targets are now standard in mortgage and real estate marketplaces. The system enforces them through routing. The rep who responds within the window gets the next lead. The rep who doesn't drops in the rotation.
- **Which Rep Gets the Lead:** Round-robin distribution is gone in most serious industries, replaced by closer-history-weighted routing. The reps who close best on certain lead types get more of those lead types. The reps who fail get fewer leads and of lower quality. The wash-out curve from Chapter 12 has not

softened in the algorithmic era. It has steepened. The system makes the math more pitiless, not less.

- **Whether the Lead Reaches a Human at All:** In many industries now, AI-powered qualification systems handle the first three or four touches before the lead is ever escalated to a working rep. The human you meet has already self-qualified across multiple interactions with the system. You are meeting an already-warmed lead. The cold prospecting that used to define commissioned work has largely disappeared at scale, replaced by a different kind of work entirely—with humans responding well and fast to leads that arrive prescored.

This is the part of the new world that reps with twenty years of experience often resist. The hustle changed. The territory changed. The judgment calls the rep used to make are now being made before the lead reaches them.

The reps who fight this lose. The reps who learn to work inside it win.

Where Your Leverage Actually Lives Now

Once you accept that the front of the funnel is gone, the question becomes: Where is your actual leverage?

There are three places. Get these right and you win inside the new system. Get them wrong and the system grinds you down.

The First Thirty Seconds After the Lead Arrives

The algorithm delivered Dana to me. But what happened in the next half-minute was still mine. I read her file in five seconds, dialed her in another five, and was in the conversation before her browser tab had finished refreshing.

The buyer who gets a competent, present, attention-paying response inside the response window converts at multiples of the rate of the buyer who gets an auto-response. The system rewards the rep who handles those thirty seconds well by routing them more leads, and the system punishes the rep who handles them badly by routing them fewer.

The reps who used to spend the first thirty seconds of a lead on small talk no longer have those thirty seconds available. The window has compressed. The work hasn't gotten less human—it has gotten more concentrated.

The Conversation, Once It Begins

Everything Parts I and II of this book taught—reading the room, the warm-up at the new speed, the questions, the table, the story, the close—none of this has changed just because the lead arrived through a system.

Dana laughed when I told her she had thirty seconds. That laugh was the warm-up. It happened in the second sentence of the conversation because the system had compressed everything that used to happen before the conversation. The first ten seconds from Chapter 2 still matter. The mirroring, the question discipline, the reading of the silent stakeholder—all of it. The system handed me Dana with a clock running. The rest was still craft.

The algorithm delivered the buyer. The algorithm didn't host her. *Hosting* her—making her feel seen, treated as a person rather than a record in a system, given a clear path through her decision—was still my job, and it is still yours.

The Feedback Loop You Give the System

This is the part most reps don't realize.

Every interaction you have with a delivered lead is data the algorithm learns from. The close, the walk, the follow-up, the no-show, the conversion, the rescission—all of it becomes training data for the routing system. The reps who consistently close certain types of leads get more of those leads. The reps who consistently fail with certain types get fewer of them.

You are not a passive recipient of the algorithm. You are training it, every day, with every action.

The veteran who closes carefully—who walks deals that are not real, who closes the deals that are, who handles the follow-up promises honestly—is teaching the system to send them more of the right kind of buyer. The rep who chases every lead and fails on most of them is teaching the system to send them fewer leads of the kind they can actually close.

This is the new feedback loop of the commissioned career. Your file in Chapter 11 lives in your head. Your file in Chapter 13 lives in the CRM. Your file in this chapter lives in the algorithm's training data. Three layers of the same file. All three matter. The third one decides which buyers reach your screen tomorrow morning.

The New Failure Modes

Three new ways reps fail inside an algorithmic pipeline, in addition to all the old ways:

- **Treating Leads as Commodities Because the System Delivered Them:** The rep who stops doing the deep human work because *the system already qualified the buyer* has misunderstood what the system actually did. The system filtered. The system scored. The system routed. The filtering is not the qualification. The buyer is still a person, still carrying a deeper intention that has not been executed, still needing to be hosted into a decision. The rep who treats algorithmic leads as commodities will close some of them by volume—and lose more than they should because the conversation has been short-changed.
- **Competing Against the Algorithm Instead of Working with It:** Some reps try to find workarounds. Direct outreach to bypass the system. Gaming response times. Working leads outside the official channel to avoid the routing rules. This rarely scales and almost always damages the rep's standing inside the system over time. The algorithm sees what is happening. The algorithm adjusts. The rep who tried to outsmart it ends up with fewer and worse leads, not more.
- **Failing to Respond Inside the Window:** The ninety-second window is real. The five-minute window is real. Reps who treat them as optional get sorted by the system within weeks. The veteran from Chapter 12 who survived twenty years of pure-commission selling and developed a methodical pace

can't afford that pace on an algorithmic lead. The pace is now in the system. Adapt or get sorted out.

What This Means for Managers

A short word for sales managers reading this book.

The manager used to allocate leads. Now the algorithm does. The manager used to identify which reps were best for which lead types. Now the routing system does. The manager used to be the bottleneck between the marketing department and the sales floor. The algorithm has dissolved that bottleneck.

Your role has shifted. You are now coaching reps inside an algorithmic system they are already operating in—whether you understand it or not.

The manager who does not understand how the routing system works cannot coach the rep effectively inside it. "Why didn't you close that lead?" is the wrong question if the rep's response window was missed by twenty seconds. "Why is your conversion dropping?" is the wrong question if the algorithm has been routing the rep a different kind of lead than the one they used to convert on.

Understand the system. Coach inside it. Or watch your top performers learn the system faster than you do and outearn you.

The Forward Bet

Understanding the algorithm is no longer optional for working commissioned reps.

The reps who are integrating algorithmic awareness into their daily practice today are building a compounding advantage. They are training their routing systems to send them better leads. They are responding inside the windows. They are working *with* the system rather than against it. By 2030, the reps who have built this fluency will be operating with a competitive position that unaided reps will not be able to close.

This is not theoretical. This is happening now, in every commissioned industry, at scale. The reps who recognize it now have the advantage of being early. The reps who continue to operate as if the system did not exist will be sorted out by the system itself, on a timeline shorter than they expect.

The pipeline lives in the algorithm.

The conversation lives where it always has.

The Closing Rule

The algorithm delivers the fish.

You still have to clean it, cook it, and not poison the guest.

The fish is the lead. The cooking is the conversation. The guest is the buyer—who came to you not as a record in a system but as a person with money on the line, a decision to make, and a private intention to execute.

The algorithm knows none of that. The algorithm knows the score, the route, the window. But it doesn't know the guest. It doesn't know how to host. And it doesn't know what to do when the soft pull missed a car lease and the actual DTI is three points worse than the system thought.

That is still you.

That has always been you.

The pipeline has moved. The kitchen has not.

Next chapter: The Agentic Salesperson—what happens when AI stops being an assistant and starts acting on its own, and what every working rep needs to understand about it before the next eighteen months pass.

CHAPTER 16
THE AGENTIC SALESPERSON

I called my internet provider to upgrade my plan. Nothing complicated. I needed faster speeds for trading and streaming.

The voice picked up immediately. No background noise. No call-center hum. No delay.

"I can help with that. What can I do for you?"

"What's your fastest plan?"

"Based on your usage history, the top-tier gigabit plan would reduce your latency and support multiple high-demand devices. It's our most popular option for customers working from home or trading in real time."

I paused. The response was not generic. It had used *my* usage history. It had identified *my* situation. It had positioned the recommendation around *my* specific concerns. The phrase "trading in real time" was something I had said only twenty seconds earlier.

"What's the catch?"

"A higher monthly cost and a twelve-month agreement. However, customers in your profile typically see performance improvements immediately."

I leaned back. Smiled a little.

"Are you a real person?"

A short pause. Then:

"I'm here to get you the best setup as quickly as possible."

That was the moment.

The agent didn't lie to me. It also didn't say yes. It said something different—a sentence that was true but evasive, the kind of sentence a working rep would never quite say because a working rep would either answer the question directly or laugh.

The agent did neither. It pivoted. It returned the focus to my outcome. It kept the conversation moving. It was good. It was disciplined. It was, in some ways, more efficient than the human reps I had dealt with at this company over the years.

It was also not a person. And the moment I asked the question, the agent's structural limitation became visible.

This chapter is about what that moment means for your career.

What Agentic AI Actually Is

Most working reps in 2026 still think of AI as a chatbot or a writing assistant. Something you query. Something that returns text.

Agentic AI is different.

An agent takes multi-step actions on its own. It doesn't wait for the human to drive each step. It runs a sequence—researches the buyer, drafts the outreach, sends it, monitors the response, books the meeting, prepares the rep, follows up—without asking permission at every step. The unit of work is the workflow, not the message.

An agent uses tools. It browses websites. It sends emails. It schedules meetings. It updates CRMs. It queries databases. It calls APIs. It does things in the world rather than just generating text about them.

An agent operates with judgment, within bounds set by its operator. It decides which lead to nurture and which to release. It decides whether a meeting time is acceptable. It decides when to escalate a conversation to a human and when to handle it itself.

In Chapter 14, I described AI as a partner—Iris, the assistant who synthesizes and suggests while I make the decisions. An agent is something different. An agent is closer to an employee. The rep becomes a supervisor rather than an operator.

This distinction matters more than it sounds. The relationship is different. The skills required to use AI agents well are different from the skills required to use AI assistants well. And the implications for the working salesperson are different too.

What Agents Are Already Doing

This is not hypothetical. Agents are in production right now in every major commissioned industry. The reps and managers who are still talking about agentic AI as a future technology are about to be surprised.

- **Outreach:** Autonomous sequencing systems conduct multistep email and SMS campaigns, adapt their cadence to recipient behavior, and route warm responses to human reps. In B2B sales, in mortgage origination, in real estate brokerage, in insurance, and in financial advisory work, the first three to five touches with a prospect are now routinely handled by agents before any rep is involved. Vacation ownership and the timeshare industry are not far behind. The pattern is the same across all of them—the cold layer of human work that used to consume the rep's morning has been quietly absorbed into software, and the reps using it are operating with a meaningful advantage over the reps who are not.
- **Qualification:** Chat-based systems conduct full discovery conversations with buyers, score the conversation, and either book the meeting or release the lead. The SDR layer in serious B2B operations has already been substantially absorbed by these systems.
- **Scheduling and Coordination:** Agents negotiate meeting times across multiple calendars, send reminders, reschedule when conflicts arise, and handle the entire pre-meeting logistics layer. The administrative assistant work that used to require a junior team member is now a software subscription.
- **Research and Preparation:** Agents pull buyer history, company background, market context, competitive intelligence, and recommended talking points—and deliver them to the rep as a single brief before the meeting starts. The pre-meeting prep that used to take an hour can now be generated with the click of a button.

- **Post-Meeting Administration:** Agents transcribe, summarize, update CRMs, draft follow-up messages, and queue next-action recommendations. The administrative tail after every meeting is increasingly hands-free.

I want to be specific about what this means.

If you are a working commissioned rep in 2026, the mechanical layer of your job is being eaten by agents whether you adopt them or not. The reps who are using these tools are having more conversations per day than the reps who are not. The math of the floor will sort this out within a few years.

This is the part of the chapter where I do not panic, and I also do not pretend.

What Agents Cannot Do

The technology is impressive. The technology is also limited in specific ways that matter enormously for the working rep, and this section is the one I most want you to read carefully.

Agents cannot do the conversation.

Not in any meaningful sense. Not for the high-stakes decisions that buyers actually make at the consequential end of any commissioned market. The reasons are structural, and they're not going to be solved by the next model release or the next product cycle:

- **Agents Cannot Read the Room:** They can analyze sentiment in text, but they cannot feel what a buyer is holding back. They can't see the partner-look across a kitchen table. They can't notice the wedding ring being turned for the third time, the half-uncrossed leg, the silent stakeholder whose veto is in the room. The five signals from Chapter 5 are invisible to any agent in production today or in the foreseeable arc of the technology.
- **Agents Cannot Host:** Hosting is the rep's distinctive work. The agent can deliver the buyer to the conversation, but the agent cannot make the buyer feel seen as a person rather than as a record in a system. The agent can't answer the safety question about the neighborhood with "I live three blocks away.

Here is my cell number. We can go look together tonight." That answer requires being a person.

- **Agents Cannot Recognize:** Recognition is the close, as Chapter 7 named it. The agent can score sentiment, but the agent cannot read the long silence after the divorce-fear revelation. The agent cannot wait, hold the space, and ask plainly for the order when the moment has arrived. The closing moment is internal. The agent has no internal.
- **Agents Cannot Be Accountable:** The deal that went wrong. The mistake the rep made. The apology that has to carry weight. The agent cannot do this work. The rep who lets an agent attempt it commodifies the relationship in ways the agent itself cannot detect. The buyer feels it. The buyer remembers it. The reputation that took years to build does not survive many of these.

There is a deeper structural point underneath all four of these limitations.

The work that has the highest economic value in commissioned selling—the conversation that closes the consequential deal—is exactly the work agents are worst at. This is not a coincidence. It's the structural truth of what humans and machines are currently for. The mechanical layer is being absorbed because the mechanical layer was always machinable. The human layer is surviving because the human layer was never machinable in the first place—and never will be.

This isn't optimism. It's geometry.

The Internet Agent and the Closing Conversation

Go back to the internet agent for a moment.

That agent was good at its job. It identified my need. It recommended a product. It surfaced the relevant terms. It handled an objection. It kept the conversation moving toward a sale.

It also failed at one thing.

When I asked if it was a real person, it didn't answer. It pivoted. Because answering would have changed the conversation in a way the agent's bounds didn't permit, and the agent was not equipped to handle the conversation that would have followed.

A real rep, asked the same question, would have laughed and said "yeah, hi" and moved on. The conversation would have continued. The trust would have stayed intact.

But the agent couldn't laugh. It couldn't acknowledge. It couldn't be a person because it wasn't one. The structural limit was visible in two sentences.

Now imagine the same exchange with the buyer carrying a deeper intention that they haven't executed yet. The Brian who is afraid of repeating his father. The Mario and Maria who need someone to host their household decision. The Walter and Diane who need someone to tell them their dad's fear is not their fear. The Robert and Denise who need the broker to lead the room.

The agent cannot do this. The agent will not be able to do this. The agent's structural limit becomes the rep's structural moat—their enduring competitive advantage.

That is the chapter's argument compressed into one paragraph.

What This Means for the Working Rep

Three actions for working reps in 2026 and beyond:

- **Adopt Agents for the Mechanical Layer:** If you are not yet using agentic tools for outreach, scheduling, research, or administrative work, you are giving up time that should be going to conversations. The competitive cost of refusing these tools is rising every quarter. The reps who hold out the longest are the reps who get sorted out the earliest.
- **Redistribute Your Day Toward the Conversation:** As agents take the mechanical layer, your day should not stay the same with more output. Your day should change—more time on actual conversations, more time on the hard moments that require human presence, more time on the work this book has been teaching for fifteen chapters. The rep who uses agents to do more of the same work is missing the point. The rep who uses agents to free time for deeper work is taking the opportunity.

- **Become Unmistakably Human in Your Buyer-Facing Work:** Every channel a buyer uses is now flooded with AI-generated communication. The agent that called me about my internet plan was good—and it was indistinguishable from a hundred other reasonably good interactions a buyer has every week. As the channel fills with this kind of competent automation, the rep who shows up with real presence, real voice, and real stakes is increasingly distinguishable from the agents. That distinguishability is no longer optional. It's the moat.

The rep in 2030 will not be competing with other reps in the way they competed in 2020. The rep in 2030 will be competing against the question every buyer is asking themselves before they ever pick up the phone: "Do I even need a human for this?" The rep who has nothing to offer the buyer that an agent cannot offer better is the rep who will not survive that question.

The rep who has the conversation—the reading, the question, the story, the close, the hosting—has everything an agent does not.

The Honest Threat

I'm not saying the human rep is safe forever in every category.

Some sales work is on its way out. The chapter would not be honest if it did not name this. For example:

- **Low-stakes, transactional, repetitive sales work**—the kind of work that lives entirely in Quadrant 1 from Chapter 1—is mostly going. Much of it is already gone. The simple e-commerce transaction, the commodified service signup, the form-fill insurance quote, the routine product reorder. None of these required a human in the first place, and agents are absorbing what remained.
- **The bottom tier of commissioned roles in every industry** is the most exposed. The reps who were already the lowest performers—whose value-add over an automated system was marginal—are the most replaceable. The math from Chapter 12 was already pitiless. Agents make it more so. The wash-out curve is going to steepen, not flatten.

- **The entry-level training pipeline** is the part most industries have not yet figured out. Many trades built their training around having junior reps do the mechanical work—outreach, qualification, simple closes—for years before being promoted to consultative selling. Agents are eating that mechanical work. How the industry will train the next generation of closers without those stepping stones is an open question. The reps in their thirties and forties who are reading this book will probably benefit from the shift. The reps who would have started in 2030 are entering a different industry than the one their managers entered.

These are honest concerns. They don't change the chapter's central argument—the conversation survives, and the rep who can do it has an advantage that compounds every year—but they do mean the playing field will look different in five years than it does today.

The rep who understands the difference between what agents take and what agents leave is the rep who positions themselves on the right side of the curve.

The rep who refuses to look at this is the rep who finds themselves on the wrong side without knowing how they got there.

The Closing Rule

Agents take the work that the machine can do.

What's left is the work only you can do.

Make sure you can still do it.

The training didn't come from a book. It came from a thousand conversations with real buyers across real tables, learning to read the room, ask the question, tell the story, recognize the close. That work is what this book has been about. It is also what agents cannot do.

The rep who has spent the last decade hiding from those conversations—in the CRM, in the script, in the volume game—does not have what agents cannot replace. The rep who has spent the last decade building the file does.

The competitive moat is built one conversation at a time. The blank check from Chapter 12 is filled out one number at a time. The craft is older than every technology that has tried to replace it, and the craft is what is left when the technology takes everything else.

Use the agents. Adopt them. Let them eat the work that was never going to make you better at this anyway.

Then go have the conversation.

That part is still yours.

Next chapter: The Stack You Actually Need—the working tool list for a commissioned rep in 2026, what to use, what to ignore, and how to think about a tool stack that will keep evolving.

CHAPTER 17
THE STACK YOU ACTUALLY NEED

If you are a working commissioned rep reading this chapter, you already know your tools.

You know which CRM you trust. You know which one your colleagues swear by and which one you would never go back to. You know the loan origination system you use, the e-signature platform, the dialer, the lead source, the document workflow, the scheduling layer. You have opinions. You have been burned by some of these products. You have been saved by others.

This chapter is not going to tell you which specific tools to buy.

For one thing, you already know more about your industry's working stack than any book can teach you. For another, the products that matter in 2026 will not all be the products that matter in 2030. Two of the platforms I'm running today will likely be gone, acquired, or unrecognizable within five years. The same is true of yours.

What this chapter is going to do is help you think about *why* you use what you use—and what test every tool in your stack should pass.

What I Actually Run

I run about ten distinct tools across my mortgage and real estate practice in a typical week. A CRM. A loan origination system. An MLS platform. A transaction management tool. An e-signature platform.

Two distinct lead sources—one for the real estate side, one for the mortgage side. A dialer with SMS. A showing scheduler. A verification service for income and employment. A scheduling tool layered onto the standard email and chat environment.

Ten tools. I am not going to name the products. You already know your options in each category. The products I use are the result of years of trial, error, and personal fit. They may not be right for you.

What matters is not which products I picked. What matters is the *seven universal categories* every working commissioned rep needs to cover, and the *industry-specific layer* on top.

The Seven Universal Categories

Every working commissioned rep in 2026 needs tools across these seven categories. The specific products will vary. The categories themselves are stable. They will look roughly the same in 2030, even after most of today's specific products have been replaced.

- **The CRM:** Your working memory, externalized. Chapter 13 covered this.
- **The AI Synthesis Partner:** Your second brain. Chapter 14 covered this.
- **The Communications Layer:** Phone, text, email, compliant with your industry's regulatory requirements.
- **The Scheduling Layer:** Calendar coordination, meeting management, automated reminders.
- **The Document and Signature Layer:** Contracts, disclosures, signed documents.
- **The Pipeline and Lead-Routing Layer:** The algorithmic system that delivers your leads. Chapter 15 covered this.
- **The Agentic Layer:** Autonomous tools that handle multi-step work. Chapter 16 covered this. Optional in 2026, likely standard by 2028.

Seven categories—anywhere from four to seven tools depending on how many categories your products consolidate into one platform.

The Industry-Specific Layer

On top of the universal seven, your industry will require its own tools. For mortgage and real estate, four additional categories matter:

- **A loan origination system** for the mortgage side
- **An MLS platform** for the real estate side
- **A transaction management platform** for managing the document and deadline flow of a real estate transaction
- **A verification service** for income, employment, and asset checks

These four bring my working stack to ten tools. That isn't bloat. It's the actual cost of doing the work in these specific industries.

Other industries have their own equivalents. Insurance has carrier portals and quoting engines. Financial advisory has portfolio management platforms. Auto sales has DMS systems. Vacation ownership has resort inventory and contract systems. Whatever you sell, your industry layer is real, and it sits on top of the universal seven, not in place of it.

The Test

Every tool in your stack should pass one test:

Does this make you more present to the buyer, or less?

If a tool gives you back attention you can pour into the conversation, it earns its place. If a tool takes attention away from the conversation, it doesn't belong, no matter how impressive its features.

Examples of tools that obviously pass the test: the CRM that holds buyer history that you can't remember unaided, the AI that synthesizes three months of correspondence into a brief before your meeting, the e-signature platform that closes the document loop in minutes instead of days, the dialer that connects you to a buyer inside the response window. Each one returns time and clarity that go straight into the conversation.

Examples of tools that obviously fail the test: the dashboard that shows you metrics you already know, the analytics platform that requires an hour of report-building per week, the third communication channel you adopted because someone told you buyers might be there, the automation system so complex it requires its own management. Each one consumes attention without giving any back.

The middle cases are where the test does real work. A new platform looks promising. A colleague swears by it. The marketing is compelling. Run the test honestly: *If I add this, will I have more attention for the buyer, or less?* If the honest answer is *less*, the tool doesn't belong, regardless of how impressive it looks.

This is the only durable framework for evaluating tools, because it's the only framework that doesn't depend on what the tools currently look like. A tool that exists in 2030 and helps you be more present to the buyer is a good tool. A tool that exists in 2030 and pulls your attention away from the buyer is a bad tool, regardless of what the product brochure says.

Your job—when you read a product review, talk to a colleague about their stack, or evaluate a new platform—is to ask the same question every time. *Does this make me more present to the buyer, or less?*

Many tools will pass the test. Add them. Many will fail. Pass.

The Honest Reality of Product Selection

There is no perfect tool list for any commissioned industry. Reps have many choices in each category. The only way to know what works for you is to analyze your specific needs, match them to a product's features, review the ratings, talk to colleagues, and trial the tools yourself.

The ultimate satisfaction is trial.

A product that works for me in my market with my buyer profile and my brokerage requirements may be the wrong product for you in a different market with different inventory and different working conditions. The chapter cannot make these decisions for you. Your colleagues cannot make them for you. The reviews cannot make them for you. You have to try the tools and decide what fits.

What the chapter can tell you is *which categories must be covered and what test each tool has to pass.* The rest is your work.

The Audit

Before you finish this chapter, run a quick audit. List every tool you currently use in a typical week. Include the ones your firm pays for that you barely touch. For each one, write one sentence explaining how it makes you more present to the buyer. The tools where you can't finish the sentence are the tools to cut.

Most working reps will find at least two that fail honestly, and many will find more. Cutting them recovers cognitive load, subscription budget, and time—all of which can go back into the conversations the tools were supposed to be supporting.

Run the audit again in twelve months. The stack should keep getting leaner, not heavier.

What This Will Look Like in 2030

If you are reading this chapter in 2030, most of the specific products I am using in 2026 are gone or different. Some have been acquired. Some have been displaced. Some have been replaced by agentic systems that consolidated multiple categories into one platform. The CRM that was best-in-class in 2026 is probably not the CRM that is best-in-class in 2030.

That is the nature of working in commissioned sales in this era. The tools change. The reps who adapt to whatever the current stack looks like—without getting attached to any specific product—will operate effectively across that change. The reps who become loyal to a specific platform will spend their careers retraining themselves.

The categories will remain. The principle will remain. The conversation will remain.

Stay flexible on the products. Stay rigorous on the principle.

What the Tools Cannot Do

This is the only part of the chapter that matters more than the rest.

The tools deliver the buyer to you. The tools prepare you for the meeting. The tools follow up after the meeting. The tools track the pipeline, hold the history, organize the documents, schedule the next conversation. The tools are real. They are valuable. They are here to stay, and they will only get better.

But the tools do not produce the signature.

The signature happens at a table. Or in a kitchen. Or on a phone call when both parties are present, attention undivided. It happens when a human buyer trusts a human rep enough to commit money, time, and risk to a decision the buyer was already carrying but had not yet executed.

The CRM can hold every detail about the buyer. But the CRM cannot sit across from them at the table.

The AI assistant can prepare the perfect briefing. But the AI assistant cannot read the partner-look or hear the catch in the voice.

The lead-routing algorithm can deliver a scored prospect to your screen in ninety seconds. But the algorithm cannot host the buyer through their decision.

The agentic system can handle the entire pre-meeting workflow autonomously. But the agent cannot be the person sitting across from the buyer when the moment arrives.

All of these tools exist to bring you to one place—across from a buyer with a decision to make.

Picture the moment. The documents are on the table. The buyer's pen is in their hand. The technology has done its work—the lead found you, the prep happened, the CRM is updated, the e-signature platform is open and waiting. What's happening in that moment is older than every tool in your stack. The buyer is looking for one thing before they sign. They are looking at *you.* They are checking, in some part of themselves they may not even be aware of, whether they trust the person across from them enough to commit.

Once you are in that room, your stack is over. Your training is over. Your prep is over. There is only you, the buyer, the question they are carrying, and the signature on the line that will tell you whether they trusted you enough to act.

That part of the work is not changing.

That part of the work is not going away.

That part of the work is what you are paid for.

The right stack is the smallest stack that lets you spend the most time face-to-face with the buyer.

Every tool you add takes attention away from the conversation. Some tools give the attention back, multiplied. Those earn their place. The rest do not.

Build the stack. Audit it. Cut what doesn't pass the test. Trial what looks promising. And remember why any of it exists.

The platforms will change.

The signature on the line will not.

Next chapter: The Honest Forecast—where the craft, the science, and the technology are going by 2030, 2035, and 2040, and what the working rep should be doing now to be on the right side of the curve.

CHAPTER 18
THE HONEST FORECAST

This is the closing chapter of the book.

It is also the only chapter where I have to talk about a future I cannot actually see.

Every business book ends here. The author who has spent two hundred pages explaining the present arrives at the chapter where they predict the next ten years. Most of these chapters age badly. The forecast was wrong. The technology turned somewhere unexpected. The author's predictions, written with such confidence in their moment, turned out to be the part of the book the reader can safely skip.

I want to do this chapter differently.

I am going to make three claims about the next ten years. The first one is about the technology. The second one is about the craft. The third one is about you—the working rep who has read this book to its closing chapter.

I am most confident about the third claim. The first two serve it.

What the Technology Will Probably Do

By 2030, most of the mechanical sales work in commissioned industries will be done by agents.

The reps who are currently spending their day on outreach, qualification, scheduling, and administration will look like the reps spending their day on paper notebooks in 2015. The work hasn't disappeared.

It's been absorbed into software, and the reps still doing it manually are now operating at a significant structural disadvantage.

The algorithmic routing systems will get more sophisticated. The response windows will tighten. The reps will train the systems, and the systems will train back—in a feedback loop that gets faster every year. By 2030, the rep who is not algorithmically fluent will be unemployable in serious commissioned roles.

By 2035, the stack will look very different in its specifics. Several of the platforms I named in Chapter 17 will be gone or unrecognizable. Categories will have consolidated. New categories will have emerged. The agentic layer that is optional in 2026 will be the central layer in 2035, and what looked like agents in 2026 will look like primitive automation by then.

By 2040, I am not going to pretend to know what the stack looks like. Anyone who tells you they know what business technology looks like fifteen years out is selling something. I will not be one of them.

That is the technology forecast. It's short because it has to be. The chapter is not about the technology. The technology is the backdrop.

What the Craft Will Not Do

The craft will not change.

I want to be specific about what I mean by this, because it's the most important claim in the chapter.

The buyer will still arrive at the conversation carrying a decision they have not yet executed. The job to be done has not changed since the first transaction in human history. People want things. People are afraid of the wrong choice. People need someone to host them through the decision. The technology around the conversation has changed every decade for the last fifty years, but the conversation itself has not.

The room will still be a room. By 2030, the room may be a Zoom window. By 2035, the room may be a virtual environment we cannot yet picture. By 2040, the room may be something else entirely. *It will still be a room.* Two people. Attention undivided. The smaller signals that decide deals. The partner-look. The wedding-ring pause. The catch in the voice. The silence after the hard question.

The signature will still be a human act. By 2030, the signature may be biometric. By 2035, it may be done through an interface I cannot describe. The act of commitment—the moment when a buyer chooses to take on the risk of action—is internal to the buyer. The form changes. The act does not.

The conversation, in other words, will not be absorbed by the technology. The conversation is what the technology is trying to make better, faster, more frequent. The conversation is what every tool in your stack exists to deliver you to. The conversation is the work the buyer is paying for, whether they know it or not.

When everything else is optimized, the only edge left is human connection.

Automation scales.

Connection is what closes.

What the Veteran Knows

I want to tell you something now that is the deepest argument in this book.

A veteran rep—a working closer who has spent fifteen, twenty, twenty-five years in rooms with real buyers across real tables—develops a recognition that cannot be taught from any book, including this one. The recognition cannot be encoded into an algorithm. The recognition cannot be replicated by any agent trained on a million successful closes. The recognition lives in a part of the rep that took years of toil to build.

The veteran knows when to ask for the money.

Not from analysis. Not from a script. Not from a checklist the rep is running in their head. The veteran knows in their body. Something in the room shifts—a third sigh, a partner's nod, the slight change in posture, the way the silence sits differently now than it did two minutes ago—and the veteran's nervous system fires before the conscious mind catches up. *Ask for the money. The moment has arrived. Don't go past the close.*

This is the craft compressed into its smallest unit. The veteran's brain has watched a thousand closes. The veteran's body has felt a thousand rooms shift. Over years, the veteran's nervous system has built a pattern-recognition system that operates faster than thought. The moment arrives. The veteran asks. The buyer signs. The veteran could not, if you asked them afterward, fully explain how they knew. They just knew.

I want to be honest with you about what an algorithm trained on a million conversations can do, and what it cannot do.

The algorithm can learn what successful closes look like in retrospect. It can score sentiment. It can recognize verbal patterns associated with high conversion. It can build models of what buyers tend to do at certain stages of certain kinds of deals.

The algorithm cannot stand in the room at the moment when the buyer's third sigh, the partner's small nod, and the wedding ring's pause mid-twist all happen in the same half-second and *know*, without thinking, that this is when to close.

That recognition lives only in the rep who has spent the years.

It's somatic. It's built into the body. It is the file from Chapter 11, embodied. It is the reason Joe could close deals that other reps could not. It is the reason the veteran on the floor is worth more than any tool the platform vendors are selling.

This recognition can only be built one way. Face-to-face. Across a table. With real buyers carrying real decisions. The reps spending their careers behind screens, working pipelines they never close in person, building stacks they never deploy in rooms—they will not develop this recognition. They cannot. The technology will not give it to them. Only the years will.

This is the deepest answer to the question of why the human rep survives in an era of optimization.

The veteran's body knows things no algorithm can.

And the buyer, in the moment of decision, can tell.

What You Should Do Now

Three things, for the rep reading this in 2026 or 2030 or whenever the chapter finds you:

- **Learn the Craft:** The book has been teaching the craft for seventeen chapters. Internalize it. Practice it across actual buyers in actual conversations. The conversation is the only training that builds the recognition the veteran has. The reps who learn the craft will have a career. The reps who learn the tools but not the craft will not.

- **Adopt the Tools:** Without panicking. Without chasing every new platform. Without resisting either. Run the audit from Chapter 17. Build the working stack. Use the tools to free time for more conversations, not fewer. By 2030, the rep who refused to adopt the tools will have been sorted out. By 2030, the rep who adopted the tools without learning the craft will also have been sorted out. Both groups will lose. Only the rep who did both will be working in 2030.
- **Build the File:** The file from Chapter 11. The accumulated evidence of doing the work under pressure. The file does not depreciate. The file does not become obsolete. The file is the only asset the working rep has that the technology cannot take. It is built one conversation at a time, over years, and by 2030, the reps who have been building it consistently will have a competitive moat that didn't exist a decade earlier.

These three things are the whole of what you can do. They are also enough.

What I Am Less Sure About

A short list of things I don't know:

- **How the Entry-Level Training Pipeline Will Work:** The mechanical work that taught new reps the craft is being eaten by agents. How the industry will train the next generation of closers—the next generation of veterans whose nervous systems will need to be built one room at a time—is unclear. I don't know what happens when the apprenticeship system erodes faster than the industry can replace it.
- **How the Wash-Out Curve Will Evolve:** The algorithmic sorting will probably steepen it. The migration of mechanical work to agents may compress it. The curve will not disappear, but I don't pretend to know its exact shape.

- **What Categories Will Emerge That This Book Didn't Anticipate:** Chapter 17 named seven universal categories. In 2030, there may be eight. There may be six. Some of the categories may consolidate in ways I can't picture.
- **What 2040 Looks Like:** I'm being honest with you. Nobody knows what 2040 looks like. The book makes claims about 2030 that it can defend. It's more cautious about 2035—and silent about 2040.

This is the chapter telling you what it doesn't know.

You should trust the rest of the chapter more because of this section, not less.

A Working Broker in 2032

Let me close with an image.

It is sometime in 2032. The platforms have consolidated. The agentic layer is doing what was unimaginable in 2026. Lead generation, qualification, scheduling, research, post-meeting administration—all of it is happening autonomously. The working broker's day looks completely different than it looked when this book was written.

The broker is sitting across from a buyer.

The table is the same as the tables in Chapter 5. The buyer is a real person carrying a real decision. The conversation happening in the room is the conversation this book has spent seventeen chapters teaching. The technology has delivered the buyer to this moment. The technology has prepared the broker for this meeting. The technology has done everything it can do.

The broker is reading the room. The buyer is at the edge of decision. The broker's body—the body that has spent years building the file, one conversation at a time—recognizes that the moment has arrived.

The broker asks for the order.

The buyer signs.

What happened in that room is what has happened in rooms like it for as long as humans have made consequential decisions in each other's presence. Every chapter of this book has been about that moment. Every tool in the broker's stack served to bring them to it. Every algorithm and agent in their workflow exists to make more of these moments possible.

The technology will keep changing. The room will not.

The signature on the line will always require a human across from a human. Whatever else the next decade brings, that part of the work is yours. The veteran's body knows what no algorithm can. The conversation is what closes. The craft is what survives.

Build the file. Adopt the tools. Show up in the room.

Make sure you are still able to be there when the moment arrives.

— *Dave Dass*

FIELD REFERENCE

The book you have just read is the long version of what veteran closers do. This section is the short version. Use it before the tour. Use it after a stalled deal. Use it when you're training a newer rep and you don't have time to walk them through the whole book.

Each entry is short. Each one points back to the chapter where the full treatment lives.

Photograph these pages. Text them to other reps. Tape them inside a binder. Field manuals get used—so should this one.

I. Before the Conversation

Know Your Quadrant (Ch. 1)

- **Transactional sale.** One coherent decision window. Buyer arrives in one frame of mind. Deal lives or dies inside that frame.
- **Complex sale.** Has to survive time. Multiple meetings. Multiple stakeholders. Multiple frames.
- The axis is not small versus large. It's transactional versus complex. Forty years of training got this wrong.
- Identify the quadrant before you walk in. The playbook is different for each.

The Pre-Tour State Audit (Ch. 2)

- **Energy.** Am I bringing it? If not, what's in the way?
- **Posture.** Am I open or closed? Reset what's closed.
- **Breath.** Shallow or deep? Five slow breaths if shallow.
- **Focus.** Am I here, or am I still in the last thing?
- Thirty seconds of audit before the door opens. Most reps skip it. The ones who run it build a structural advantage that compounds across a career.

Reading the Parking Lot (Ch. 2)

- The tour starts before the customer opens the car door.
- Watch the posture in the driver's seat before they get out.
- Watch who walks ahead and who lags behind.
- Watch for the watch check, the phone glance, the dentist-office face.
- By the time you shake their hand, you should already know how to run the next ninety minutes.

Choosing the Version of Yourself the Buyer Needs (Ch. 2)

- A young couple needs warm and welcoming.
- A retired executive needs precise and credible.
- A family with three kids in chaos needs calm and steady.
- You are not changing who you are. You are choosing which true version of yourself to bring forward.

II. The First Ten Seconds

The Buyer Is Reading You Before You Say a Word (Ch. 2)

- Posture, handshake, eye contact, name memory, who you address first—all of it is data the buyer is processing.
- The first ten seconds set a ceiling. Most of the rest of the conversation runs under that ceiling.
- Treat the lot, the lobby, the hallway, the handshake as part of the sale. Because they are.

The Handshake as Information (Ch. 2)

- Firm but not crushing. Web meets web. Eye contact while connected.
- Use the buyer's name in the first sentence after the handshake breaks.
- Notice their grip. Tight, weak, hesitant, confident—that tells you how they walk into rooms.
- Notice the eye contact. Held or broken—that tells you how they expect to be treated.

Mirroring Before Mirroring (Ch. 2)

- Match pace, posture, energy without thinking. The veteran's mirror is unconscious.
- Slow couple, slow pace. Quiet family, quiet voice. Match the room before you lead it.
- The technical mirror (repeating the last few words) is downstream of the deeper one (paying attention).
- The buyer can feel the difference between a mirror that comes from attention and one that comes from technique.

III. The Warm-Up

The Three Categories of Warm-Up Questions (Ch. 3)

- **Where are you from?** Geography, travel context, what kind of trip this has been so far. Listen for the energy reserves they have for the next ninety minutes.
- **What does life look like back home?** Work, family, daily reality. This is where the kids' names come up. The richest information.
- **What kind of vacations have you taken before?** Their reference points for what ownership could mean. What they have loved. What they have postponed.

The Fourth Question—the One You Don't Ask (Ch. 3)

- Budget. Income. Credit. Whether they're ready to buy today.
- Asked in the warm-up, these signal that you've arrived at the pitch before the rapport has been earned.
- The buyer's body language closes the moment they hear them. Save them for later.

Specific vs. Generic Compliments (Ch. 3)

- Generic compliments are withdrawals from the trust account. "Nice shirt" costs you.
- Specific compliments are deposits. "That's a great watch—is that vintage?" earns.
- The difference is whether the compliment proves you were paying attention.
- If nothing specific surfaces, no compliment. Silence beats a generic compliment.

Where the Warm-Up Ends—the Four Signals (Ch. 3)

- The buyer asks a question about the product without being prompted.
- Body language opens—uncrossed arms, leaning in, sustained eye contact.
- The buyer makes a joke or volunteers personal information unprompted.
- The buyer says some version of "So, tell me more about . . ."
- When you see any one of these, move. Before then, don't.

IV. The Questions

Rackham's Four (Ch. 4)

- **Situation.** Context. Use sparingly. Buyers tire fast.
- **Problem.** Surface the pain. Requires trust to be built first.
- **Implication.** What does the problem cost? *The single most underused question type in modern sales.*
- **Need-payoff.** What would it look like if the problem were solved? Let the buyer paint the picture.

Family A—Truth Questions (Ch. 4)

Surface what the buyer is hiding.

- **The opener.** "What's keeping you from saying yes today?" Direct, no softener. Highest confidence required.
- **The isolator.** "Other than affordability, is there anything else keeping you from saying yes today?" Used when money has entered the conversation. Separates it from everything else.
- **The soft isolator.** "Other than money, what else would stop you from moving forward?" Gentler. Used when the buyer is more guarded.

Family B—Conditional Closes (Ch. 4)

Neutralize the named obstacle. Ask for a contingent commitment.

- **The structural close.** "If we could structure your ownership comfortably within your budget, would we move forward today?" Most flexible.
- **The payment close.** "Assuming we can get the payment where it needs to be, are we ready to do this?" Narrows to one variable.
- **The number close.** "What if I told you we could make this work at $X—would we have a deal?" Most aggressive. Use sparingly.

Family C—Identity Audits (Ch. 4)

The rare move. The buyer has volunteered identity-level resistance. You ask them to weigh it against another part of their own identity.

- "Is your fear of becoming X bigger than your commitment to Y?"
- Only available when the buyer has disclosed an identity-level objection unprompted.
- Used wrong, becomes manipulation. Used right, reaches a level no other question can.
- Used a handful of times across an entire career. Not a tool for casual deployment.

The Pause After the Question (Ch. 4)

- After a real question, wait.
- Wait longer than is comfortable.
- Let the buyer fill the silence.
- The veteran sits in five seconds. The rookie can't sit in two.
- The pause is where the deal lives.

V. Reading the Table

The Four Diagnostic Signals (Ch. 5)

- **The glance.** Who looks at whom before answering? That tells you the hierarchy.
- **The phone.** Held but not used. The buyer is mentally consulting someone not in the room.
- **The name test.** Who uses your name and who refuses to? The one who refuses has not accepted you as a peer yet.
- **The body geometry.** Who is closed when the other is open? Who pulls back when the other leans in?

The Talker Is Rarely the Deal (Ch. 5)

- The engaged person is usually the advocate. The advocate already wants to buy.
- The skeptic is the deal. The skeptic is quieter. Watching. Reserving judgment.
- Address the conversation to the deal, not to the talker.

Identifying the Silent Stakeholder (Ch. 5)

- Not always the spouse. Sometimes the parent. The adult child. The accountant. The business partner.
- Sometimes not in the room. The absent stakeholder whose voice is in the room because the buyer is anticipating their reaction.

The Four Moves for Including Without Forcing (Ch. 5)

- **Address the silent stakeholder by name, in passing, with new information**—without requiring them to answer.
- **Tell a story about a silent partner who became an advocate.** Third-party social proof aimed at them.
- **Slow down when the silent partner shifts.** Match their pace. The room's center of gravity is now where they are.
- **The direct invitation, used sparingly.** "What's been going through your mind as we've been talking?" Asked too early, it lands wrong. Asked at the right moment, it's one of the strongest moves you have.

The Absent Stakeholder Is Real (Ch. 5)

- "I need to talk to my husband / accountant / dad" is not a stalling tactic. It's the truth.
- Don't try to overcome the absent stakeholder. Arm the buyer with the specific information the absent stakeholder will need to bless the deal.
- One of the most powerful moves in commercial selling. Almost no rep makes it.

VI. The Story

Facts Persuade, Stories Convert (Ch. 6)

- The brain remembers narrative. It forgets data.
- The salesperson who builds his career on product knowledge builds it on something that erodes by the time the buyer reaches the parking lot.
- The salesperson who builds his career on stories builds it on something the buyer carries into the next conversation, and the next.

The Four-Part Structure (Ch. 6)

- **Setup.** Who is the protagonist? What is their situation? Two or three sentences.
- **Stakes.** What is at risk? What did the protagonist stand to lose?
- **Turn.** The decision or event that changed the trajectory.
- **Resolution.** What changed for them as a result.
- Skip any one and the story becomes an anecdote. Anecdotes are forgettable.

The Three Stories Every Salesperson Tells (Ch. 6)

- **About yourself.** Why are you doing this work? Short. Told once. Ninety seconds.
- **About the product.** Not the features. Why the product exists. What it was built to solve.
- **About them.** The story is told as if about another buyer. The buyer recognizes themselves in the protagonist. The recognition is the conversion.

The Line Between Selling and Bullshitting (Ch. 6)

- A true story shared honestly is an act of mutual recognition.
- A fabricated story is a lie engineered to produce an outcome. The buyer's instinct can almost always tell.
- Stay as close to true as possible. Every drift toward fabrication is a withdrawal from a long-term account.
- The buyer's emotional response to a true story is data, not manipulation.

VII. The Close

The Five Closing Signals (Ch. 7)

- **The leaned-back posture.** Forward equals deliberating. Back equals decided.
- **The look between partners.** A long, calm look without language is almost always the household decision being silently made.
- **The volunteered logistical question.** "How long does the paperwork take?" The buyer is pre-living the post-close moment.
- **Relaxation of guarded body language.** Uncrossed arms. Released shoulders. A small smile that wasn't there ten minutes ago.
- **The silence after a substantive question.** Long. Deliberate. Almost always precedes a yes that has not yet been articulated.

The Three Plain Asks (Ch. 7)

- **The plain ask.** "If this works for you, we have a deal. Are we doing this?"
- **The assumptive close, used correctly.** "How would you like to handle the deposit today?" When you have read that the decision has been made and the conversation is now about implementation.
- **The food-from-the-table ask.** "If this monthly payment is within your budget, and it doesn't take food from the table, are you our new owners?" The ethical close. Tells the family you would rather they walk than sign something that hurts them.

When the Moment Doesn't Arrive (Ch. 7)

- Don't force it. A forced close today is a rescission tomorrow.
- Name the absence honestly. "I don't think we're at a yes today. What would have to be different for this to be one?"
- A clean walk is sometimes the gift of the conversation.
- The buyer who is respected at a stalled close comes back. The buyer who is pressured does not.

Closing Is Recognition, Not Technique (Ch. 7)

- The moment is the move. The line is the formality.
- If you can read the room, you don't need a technique. If you can't read the room, no technique will save you.
- The veteran's close is whenever the moment arrives. The rookie's close is at minute eighty-eight regardless.

Never Prejudge. You Have Nothing. (Ch. 6)

- After an hour with a family, you don't have "nothing." You have an hour of human contact with people who showed up at the resort because some part of them wanted what we sell.
- Whether they will buy today, you cannot know. Whether they can buy today, you don't get to decide. They get to decide.
- Your job is to bring in a closer when you have run out of road, not to sign the tour out for them because you decided they were done.

VIII. The Voss Toolkit (Ch. 10)

Labeling

- "It sounds like . . ." / "It seems like . . ." / "It looks like . . ."
- Name the buyer's emotion or concern out loud, before they have to.
- Label rarely. Each label has to be earned by actual attention.
- A label that is run mechanically reads as artifice and loses its power.

Mirroring

- Repeat the last few words back. "You need to think about it?"
- The mirror invites the buyer to keep talking. To explain. To unpack.
- Most buyers fill the silence after a mirror with information they hadn't planned to share.

Calibrated Questions

- Open-ended. Start with *how* or *what.*
- "What would have to be true for this to work for you?"
- The burden of solving the problem moves to the buyer. The buyer ends up doing your work for you.

The Accusation Audit

- Name the worst version of what the buyer is probably thinking. Put it on the table first.
- "You're probably worried I'm going to spend the next hour trying to upsell you on something you don't need."
- Defuses the objection by naming it. Unnamed objections are dangerous. Named ones are workable.
- One of the most underused moves in consumer sales.

"That's Right" vs. "You're Right"

- "You're right" is dismissal. The buyer is making you stop talking.
- "That's right" is recognition. The buyer has seen themselves in something you said.
- The buyer doesn't always say the words. Read the recognition in the body, the silence, the look between partners.

IX. The Challenger Discipline (Ch. 9)

The Five Rep Profiles

- **Challenger.** Pushes back. Disagrees when the buyer is wrong. Comfortable with constructive tension. Top performer.
- **Lone Wolf.** Gut-driven. Hard to manage. Often produces. Second-best performer.
- **Hard Worker.** Reliable middle. Runs the script. Hits average numbers.
- **Reactive Problem Solver.** Customer-service rep. Solves what is asked. Polite, helpful.
- **Relationship Builder.** Friendly. Liked. Worst-performing profile.

The Four Things a Challenger Does

- **Teaches the buyer about themselves.** Not the product. Not the market. The buyer's own situation.
- **Takes control of the conversation.** Structurally, not aggressively. The flow is the rep's. The decision is the buyer's.
- **Is willing to disagree.** Calmly. Honestly. "That's not actually what would happen if you waited."
- **Asks the hard question and sits with it.** The Family A questions, deployed by someone not afraid of the answer.

The Relationship Builder Trap

- Buyers don't buy from reps they like. They buy from reps they respect.
- Liking is a social emotion. Respect is a competence emotion. They don't always travel together.
- Respect requires moments of constructive tension. The Relationship Builder cannot do this. The reflex is too strong.
- The fix is not a personality change. The fix is adding tension on top of warmth. Both can coexist.

Warmth and Tension Together

- The Challenger is *more* on the buyer's side than the Relationship Builder is.
- The Challenger is willing to tell the buyer the truth. The Relationship Builder is willing to comfort the buyer.
- The buyer feels the difference, even when they cannot name it.

X. For Sales Managers

Reading Your Floor's Five Profiles

- Most floors have all five profiles in roughly the distribution Dixon and Adamson found.
- Your top closers are Challengers and Lone Wolves. Your middle is Hard Workers and Reactive Problem Solvers. Your wash-outs are Relationship Builders.
- This isn't personal. It's structural. The fix for the Relationship Builder is technique, not character.

Coaching the Relationship Builder

- Don't tell them to stop being friendly. The warmth is a feature.
- Teach them the hard question. The pushback. The willingness to say what the buyer doesn't want to hear.
- One disagreement per ten conversations is the starting target. The math will move.

When to Walk a Tour Out (Ch. 6)

- A rep who says "I have nothing" after an hour with a family has spent an hour with people who showed up because they wanted what you sell.
- Walk the table. Ask what the rep actually said. Ask what they noticed about the family.
- Most of the time, the deal is alive and the rep doesn't see it.

When to Bring in a Closer (Ch. 6)

- A rep who has built rapport and stalled on the math is exactly the right moment for a closer.
- Give the rep a script to transfer the table with dignity. Don't embarrass them in front of the family.
- Close the deal in front of them when you can. Watching is how the next generation learns.

The Food-From-the-Table Rule (Ch. 6)

- The deal has to be small enough that it doesn't take food from the table.
- If it's bigger than that, you're not closing a deal—you're hurting a family.
- The family will find their way back to the truth eventually. And they will hurt you back. Through rescission. Bad word of mouth. The slow, quiet kind of damage that erodes a reputation across years.
- This is the line that distinguishes the closer from the predator.

XI. On Surviving the Career (Ch. 12)

The Blank Check

- Every morning, you show up to a paycheck with no number on it. At the end of the day, you write the number yourself, with whatever you closed.
- No sale, no money. The check resets to zero every morning.
- The freedom and the weight are the same object. The reason the income is uncapped is that there is no floor.
- The calculation never fully shuts off. It follows you home, on weekends, on the rare vacation you let yourself take.

The Efficiency Ratio

- Every floor runs on math. Deals per month. Tours versus closes. A closing percentage you have to maintain.
- The rep who cannot hit the number is gone in a short period. Not because anyone hates them but because the math doesn't negotiate.
- Once a rep slips below the ratio, the slide is usually in one direction. The pressure makes the closing worse, which makes the ratio worse.

The Base Is a Runway, Not a Destination (Ch. 12)

- Salary-plus-commission gives the rookie a thin floor to learn on. It buys them time to find out if the career is for them.
- The base keeps the lights on while you learn. The commission is where the living is made.
- The rep who settles into the comfort of the base and stops fighting for the close has only delayed the conversation about the ratio.

More Leave Than Stay

- For every rep who lasts at least five years, ten come and go.
- The wash-out is the rule. The survivor is the exception.
- The ones who leave didn't fail as people. They failed to write a real number on a blank check, often enough, for long enough. That's a different thing from being a failure.

Why the Survivors Survive

- Not luck. Across decades, the luck averages out.
- The craft is not just how you win. The craft is how you survive.
- The rep who masters the craft closes often enough that the check is rarely zero. That is the whole difference.

Keep the Check Separate from Your Soul

- The number you write at the end of the day measures that day's work. It does not measure your worth as a person.
- The reps who keep those two things separate survive with their souls intact.
- The reps who let the blank check become a daily referendum on whether they are worth anything get hurt, whether they close or not.
- The craft keeps you fed. Keeping the check separate from your soul keeps you whole. You need both to last.

The Honest Accounting

- The reward is real. Homes owned outright. Kids put through college without loans. A living with no ceiling, paid in full for exactly what you are worth.
- The cost is real too. The pressure finds the body. The career also leaves marks on the ones who succeed at it, not only the ones who fail.
- Both are true at the same time. Anyone who tells you only the upside is selling the dream. Anyone who tells you only the cost is selling the fear.

XII. The Other Side of the Table (Ch. 8)

What the Buyer Is Actually Doing

- Most buyers don't need to be convinced. They need help executing a decision they were already privately carrying.
- The buyer who looks resistant is often, internally, much closer to yes than the rep realizes.
- What they're resisting is not the deal. It's the pressure, the performance, the sense of being acted upon.
- Your job is to create the room within which a private intention can become a public decision.

The Pre-Arrival State

- Most buyers walk in carrying a deeper intention they have not yet executed. A trip with aging parents. An upgrade they have outgrown but never named. A home they have been quietly considering. A move they have been postponing.
- Read for the intention. The intention is what closes. The product is the structure within which the intention can finally happen.
- The buyer's bravado in the parking lot ("We're not buying today") is usually about defending against pressure, not about the actual decision.

What Buyers Wish Reps Would Do

- Trust that they are adults who know their own lives.
- Stop performing persuasion at them when they need structure to execute.
- Let them set the pace, especially on complex deals.
- Help them see what they're not seeing, not what they've already decided.

What Buyers Wish Reps Would Not Do

- Pressure them. The buyer who is ready doesn't need pressure. And the buyer who is not ready can't be pressured into it without rescission.
- Treat their resistance as something to overcome. The resistance is usually a defense against being acted upon, not a real objection to the deal.
- Run techniques on them in registers they can feel.
- Confuse a question they ask politely with the real thing they are weighing.

Recognition, Not Decision

- For most closing moments, the buyer is not deciding. The buyer is recognizing.
- The private decision was usually made before the closing moment. The signature is the artifact.
- Watch for "That just makes sense" or "We already knew." Those are recognition lines.

Long-Cycle Deals

- The close happens in the *middle* of the process, not at the signature.
- At some unspecified moment, the buyer privately decides the deal is going to happen as long as you don't stop showing up.
- After that moment, everything is paperwork. Before it, no amount of paperwork will produce a close.
- Follow-through is the most underrated single move in long-cycle work. "You stayed in it the whole time" is a deeper compliment than buyers usually receive in a sales book.

The Math Collapses the Story

- Most buyers are comparing the wrong things. The cost of the new payment to their current payment. The price to their savings. The comfort of the decision to the comfort of not making it.
- The veteran helps them see what they're actually comparing—and gives them the math that lets a private intention become a public decision.
- "Once we saw the numbers, it stopped feeling unrealistic" is the line buyers say after the story they were telling themselves collapses.

Cialdini, from the Buyer's Side

- **Reciprocity** is felt as *recognition* that the rep treated them as a person, not as gratitude or obligation.
- **Social proof** in households often comes from each other, not from outside buyers. The grandfather giving permission. The wife giving permission. The internal household proof.
- **Authority** is in the math, not in the rep. The rep is an interpreter of authority.
- **Liking** is the canon's name for what the floor calls *respect.* They are not the same thing.
- **Scarcity** rarely appears in buyer recall as a decision factor. Treat it as the weakest principle in consumer sales.
- **Unity**—the shared-identity principle—is, for households, the principle. Cialdini undersold it.

The Single Test

- Before you say anything to the buyer, ask yourself, "Am I trying to move them? Or am I helping them execute what they already brought in?"
- The first question is the rookie's question. The second is the veteran's.
- The veteran's craft is not persuasion. The veteran's craft is honoring the intention the buyer was already carrying.

XIII. On Tools—From the CRM to the Stack (Ch. 13, 14, 15, 16, and 17)

The Principle That Runs Through Every Tool You'll Ever Use

- The tool serves the craft. Never the other way around.
- The CRM is not the point. The conversation is the point.
- AI is not the point. The conversation is the point.
- Every tool that comes after this one will not be the point either. The conversation has always been—and will always be—the point.

What the CRM Is For (Ch. 13)

- The CRM is your working memory, externalized. It holds what no working rep can hold unaided across a hundred active relationships.
- Use the CRM enough to support the next conversation, and not a minute more.
- Update quickly. Notes are for your future self, not for the manager's audit.
- The buyer should never know you're using a CRM. They should only experience a rep who remembers everything that matters to them.

The CRM Trap

- Reps stall at a stage in the pipeline because they have been doing administrative work to avoid the conversation work.
- Updating fields is easy. Logging activities is easy. Picking up the phone and asking the hard question is hard.
- If your numbers aren't moving, check honestly whether you have been hiding in the CRM.

What AI Is For (Ch. 14)

- AI is a preparation engine. Pre-meeting synthesis. Pattern recognition across your own history. Real-time research on long-cycle deals. Post-meeting summary.
- Use AI to free your attention. Then put the attention where it has always belonged—in the room with the buyer.
- AI surfaces patterns that the unaided brain can't hold. The veteran reads the patterns and decides what to do with them.

The Five AI Damages

- **False confidence.** AI gives you confidence that the room doesn't support because AI cannot feel the room. The pattern says one thing. The phone call would have told you the truth.
- **Relationship damage.** AI-written messages sound clean and feel hollow. Buyers feel the difference. The rep whose communication has been outsourced to AI looks like every other rep.
- **Laziness.** Working from AI summaries without the underlying material thins the conversation. The detail you need to close is often in the source material that AI compressed away.

- **Fake apologies.** When the deal falls apart, write the apology yourself. AI cannot do accountability. The buyer feels it.
- **You stop noticing things.** This is the killer. Why listen for hesitation if AI flags sentiment? Why hold texture if AI summarizes? The slow erosion of attention is the damage that ends careers.

The AI Discipline

- **AI handles preparation. The rep handles attention.** Every use should make you *more* present to the buyer, never less.
- **Your voice never leaves you.** AI can structure and suggest. The actual words the buyer reads should always be yours, edited by you, with your attention in them.
- **AI surfaces patterns. The rep makes decisions.** Reading the room, asking the right question, recognizing the closing moment—none of this can be delegated.
- **Treat freed time as time for more conversation, not less.** The reps who use AI to expand the time they spend with buyers will outearn the reps who use it to shrink that time.

The Rule

- Use AI to prep. Never to replace your presence.
- Let it read the emails. Let it organize the noise.
- Once you're on the phone, in the car, at the table, face-to-face—put it down.
- Look people in the eye. Ask the question the machine cannot ask.
- AI doesn't close deals. People do.

The Forward Bet

- AI fluency is no longer optional for working commissioned reps.
- The reps integrating AI into preparation and synthesis today are building a compounding advantage. By the time the rest of the industry catches up, it will be standard. The reps who built the discipline early will already be ahead.
- The gap that matters is not between reps who use AI and reps who do not. That gap will close on its own.
- The gap that matters is between reps who use AI to *escape* the conversation and reps who use AI to *focus more fully* on it. That gap will widen every year for the rest of your career.

What the Algorithm Does to Your Pipeline (Ch. 15)

- The lead you used to hunt for is now delivered to you by an algorithm. Across mortgage, real estate, vacation ownership, B2B, insurance, and financial advisory, the migration is mostly complete or well underway.
- The algorithm is now making decisions you used to make: which leads are worth your time, how quickly the buyer reaches a human, which rep gets which lead, and whether the lead reaches a human at all.
- You didn't generate that lead. The system did. And the system decides whether you keep getting more of them.

The Response Window

- The ninety-second window is real. The five-minute window is real.
- The system rewards the rep who handles the window well by routing them more leads. It punishes the rep who handles it badly by routing them fewer.
- The first thirty seconds after a lead arrives is no longer optional preparation time. It's the window.
- Reps who treat the window as flexible get sorted out by the system within weeks.

Where Your Leverage Actually Lives Now

- **The first thirty seconds after the lead arrives.** The algorithm delivered the buyer. What happens next is still yours.
- **The conversation, once it begins.** Everything Parts I and II of this book taught. The system handed you the buyer. The craft is still the craft.
- **The feedback loop you give the system.** Every interaction is training data. The reps who close carefully—walking deals that aren't real, closing the ones that are—train the algorithm to send them more of the right buyers. The reps who chase every lead and fail on most of them train it to send them fewer.

The Three Layers of the File

- Your file in Chapter 11 lives in your head. The internal evidence of what you have done under pressure.
- Your file in Chapter 13 lives in the CRM. The working memory externalized.

- Your file in Chapter 15 lives in the algorithm's training data. The system that decides which buyers reach your screen tomorrow morning.
- All three matter. The third one is the one that most reps don't realize they are building, every day, with every action.

The New Failure Modes

- **Treating leads as commodities because the system delivered them.** The system filtered, but the filtering is not the qualification. The buyer is still a person who needs to be hosted into a decision.
- **Competing against the algorithm instead of working with it.** Workarounds rarely scale. The algorithm sees what is happening and adjusts. Reps who try to outsmart it end up with fewer and worse leads.
- **Failing to respond inside the window.** Those twenty seconds matter. The system sorts on this. Adapt your pace or be sorted out.

For Managers in the Algorithmic Era

- You used to allocate leads. Now the algorithm does.
- You used to identify which reps were best for which lead types. Now the routing system does.
- Your role has shifted to coaching reps inside an algorithmic system they are already operating in—whether you understand it or not.
- "Why didn't you close that lead?" is the wrong question if the response window was missed. "Why is your conversion dropping?" is the wrong question if the algorithm has been routing the rep a different kind of lead than the one they used to convert on. Understand the system or watch your top performers learn it faster than you do.

The Closing Rule for the Algorithmic Era

- The algorithm delivers the fish.
- You still have to clean it, cook it, and not poison the guest.
- The fish is the lead. The cooking is the conversation. The guest is the buyer.
- The algorithm knows the score, the route, the window. But it doesn't know the guest, and it doesn't know how to host.
- That is still you. That has always been you.
- The pipeline has moved. The kitchen has not.

What Agentic AI Actually Is (Ch. 16)

- An agent is not a chatbot. An agent takes multi-step actions without asking permission at every step.
- An agent uses tools—it browses, sends emails, schedules meetings, updates CRMs, and queries databases.
- An agent is closer to an employee than an assistant. You become a supervisor, not an operator.
- Iris from Chapter 14 was a partner. An agent is something different.

What Agents Are Already Doing

- **Outreach.** Multi-touch email and SMS sequencing, in production in B2B, mortgage, real estate, insurance, and financial advisory. The first three to five prospect touches are increasingly autonomous.
- **Qualification.** Full discovery conversations through chat, with scoring and routing handled before any rep is involved. The SDR layer is being absorbed.
- **Scheduling.** Multi-calendar coordination, reminders, rescheduling. The pre-meeting logistics layer is hands-free.

- **Research and preparation.** Buyer history, company background, competitive intelligence—delivered to the rep as a single brief, on demand.
- **Post-meeting administration.** Transcription, summary, CRM updates, follow-up drafts, next-action recommendations.

What Agents Cannot Do

- **Read the room.** Sentiment in text is not sentiment in a room. The wedding-ring twist, the half-uncrossed leg, the partner-look—all are invisible to any agent in production today.
- **Host.** The agent can deliver the buyer, but it cannot make the buyer feel seen as a person rather than a record. "I live three blocks away. Here is my cell number. We can go look together tonight"—that requires being a person.
- **Recognize.** Recognition is the close. The agent can score sentiment, but it cannot read the silence after the hard revelation, hold the space, and ask plainly for the order at the moment of arrival.
- **Be accountable.** When the deal goes wrong and an apology has to carry weight, agents cannot do this work. Buyers feel the missing accountability. Reputation doesn't survive many of these.

The Structural Truth About Machines and Humans

- The work with the highest economic value in commissioned selling—the consequential conversation—is exactly the work that agents are worst at.
- This is not a coincidence. The mechanical layer is being absorbed because the mechanical layer was always machinable. The human layer survives because the human layer was never machinable.
- The agent's structural limit is the rep's structural moat.

What the Working Rep Should Do Now

- **Adopt agents for the mechanical layer.** Outreach, scheduling, research, administrative work. The competitive cost of refusing is rising every quarter.
- **Redistribute your day toward the conversation.** Don't use agents to do more of the same work. Use them to free time for deeper work.
- **Become unmistakably human in your buyer-facing work.** As every channel fills with competent automation, the rep with real presence is increasingly distinguishable. That distinguishability is the moat.

The Honest Threat

- Low-stakes, transactional, repetitive sales work is mostly going. Quadrant 1 from Chapter 1.
- The bottom tier of commissioned roles in every industry is the most exposed. The math from Chapter 12 was already pitiless. Agents make it more so.
- The entry-level training pipeline is the part the industry hasn't figured out yet. Junior reps used to learn by doing the mechanical work that agents are now eating. How the next generation learns is an open question.
- The rep who understands which categories are going and which are surviving has a meaningful career advantage.

The Closing Rule for the Agentic Era

- Agents take the work the machine can do.
- What's left is the work only you can do.
- Make sure you can still do it.

Your Stack in 2026 (Ch. 17)

- If you are a working commissioned rep, you already know your tools. You have opinions. You know which ones earned their place and which ones did not.
- The chapter is not a product list. The book can't tell you which CRM to buy. Two years from now, half of today's specific products will be gone, acquired, or unrecognizable.
- The categories survive. The principle survives. The conversation survives.

The Seven Universal Categories

- **The CRM.** Working memory, externalized.
- **The AI synthesis partner.** Your second brain.
- **The communications layer.** Phone, text, email, compliance for your industry.
- **The scheduling layer.** Calendar coordination, meeting management.
- **The document and signature layer.** Contracts, disclosures, signed documents.
- **The pipeline and lead-routing layer.** The algorithmic system that delivers your leads.
- **The agentic layer.** Autonomous multi-step tools. Optional in 2026. Standard by 2028.

The Industry-Specific Layer

- On top of the universal seven, your industry requires its own tools.
- Mortgage and real estate add four: a loan origination system, an MLS platform, a transaction management platform, a verification service.

- Insurance, financial advisory, auto sales, and vacation ownership have their own equivalents.
- The industry layer is not bloat. It is the actual cost of doing the work in your specific industry.

The Test for Every Tool

- *Does this make you more present to the buyer, or less?*
- If a tool gives back attention that goes into the conversation, it earns its place.
- If a tool takes attention away from the conversation, it doesn't belong—regardless of how impressive its features are.
- This is the only durable framework. It doesn't depend on what the tools look like today. It doesn't depend on what they look like in 2030. It depends only on the standard the book has been making since Chapter 1.

The Audit

- List every tool you use in a typical week. Include the ones your firm pays for that you barely touch.
- For each one, write one sentence explaining how it makes you more present to the buyer.
- The tools that make you less present to the buyer are the tools to cut.
- Run the audit again in twelve months. The stack should get leaner, not heavier.

On Product Selection

- There is no perfect tool list for any commissioned industry. Reps have many choices in each category.

- The only way to know what works is to analyze your needs, match them to features, review the ratings, talk to colleagues, and trial the tools yourself.
- The ultimate satisfaction is trial.

The Closing Principle

- All of the tools exist to bring you to one place—across from a buyer with a decision to make.
- Once you're in that room, your stack is over. Your training is over. Your prep is over. There is only you, the buyer, and the signature on the line.
- The CRM can hold every detail about the buyer. It cannot sit across from them at the table.
- The platforms will change. The signature on the line will not.

A Final Word

The chapters of this book are the long version of how this craft is run.

This reference is the short version.

Neither replaces the hours.

The hours are what make you a closer. The book gives you language for what the hours have been teaching you. The reference gives you the language you can flip to under pressure.

Carry it on you the same way veterans carry the discipline that produced it.

The craft is older than every book that has been written about it. The books name what was already on the floor.

This reference is in the same spirit. It names what you have been doing—or what you've been about to learn to do—on a hundred floors across a hundred careers.

Now use it.

ACKNOWLEDGMENTS

To Jenny—none of this happens without you.

You signed up for a life with no guaranteed paycheck, long hours, weekends that were not weekends, and holidays I spent on a floor instead of at home. You never once asked me to choose something safer. You ran the life we built while I ran the floor, and you did it without complaint and without keeping score. This book exists because you made the years possible.

To Jenny and to my children—thank you for pushing me to put this down on paper. Left to myself, I might have kept it all in my head, the way the veterans before me did. You were the ones who told me the work was worth sharing, that the learning of a career belonged to more people than just me, and that I shouldn't stop until it was finished. Your encouragement is the reason there is a book at all.

To the reps, the managers, and the directors I worked alongside across forty-five years and six industries—thank you. The good ones taught me by example. The hard ones taught me by contrast. Every floor I ever stood on made me better at the work, and the craft in these pages was built shoulder to shoulder with people who lived it the same way I did.

And to the buyers—thank you most of all. You taught me more than any book ever did. Every person who sat across a table from me, carrying a real decision and trusting me to help them make it, was teaching me the craft whether either of us knew it at the time. This book is about you. It always was.

Life is like a wheel. To keep your sanity and
stay in balance, you have to keep moving.

ABOUT THE AUTHOR

Dave Dass has spent forty-five years selling—and teaching other people to sell—across six industries.

He began in manufacturing and distribution, moved through franchise restaurant operations, and spent twenty-one years as a sales director at one of the country's largest vacation ownership developers, on floors where the difference between a paycheck and a pink slip was a signature on a contract that same afternoon. Today he is a licensed real estate broker and licensed mortgage broker in Orlando, Florida, where he still sells, still closes, and still works across a table from buyers making the largest decisions of their lives.

Across those four and a half decades, he has worked as a salesperson, a manager, and a director—which means he has carried a quota, run a floor, and built the systems that other people carried quotas inside of. He has seen the craft from every seat in the room.

He holds a Bachelor's of Science degree in Business Management Studies and a certificate degree in Management Studies. The rest of his education came from the floor.

Whether You Admit It or Not is the book he wished someone had handed him at the start—and the book he believes every working salesperson (and every professional who sells without admitting it) needs now, as the technology reshaping the work arrives faster than the industry can train for it.

He lives in Orlando, Florida, with his family. He still sells.

www.ingramcontent.com/pod-product-compliance
Lightning Source LLC
LaVergne TN
LVHW100259210926
848480LV00003B/968
9798996964604